1200

KBS TOASTER OVEN AIR FRYER COMBO COOKBOOK

1200 DAYS SIMPLE HOMEMADE RECIPES ON A SMALLER SCALE

BETH DAVIS

CONTENTS

INTRODUCTION

What is the KBS Air Fryer Oven?

Air frying is a method of cooking that delivers the delicious flavor and satisfying crunch of deep-fried food but uses little to no oil to achieve those results. The way it works is that an air frying oven quickly circulates superheated air throughout the oven, cooking your food from all angles to create a crispy, fried layer and even-browning on all sides.

An air fryer oven is a full-sized oven that features an air fry cooking mode integrated within the oven cavity. With this innovative technology, you can now enjoy all of the benefits of air fry no matter what kind of range you're looking for - induction, gas, or electric. By using a high-powered fan to circulate hot air around the food at a high speed, our in-range air fry feature cooks ingredients to a perfectly crisped finish.

Eight Benefits Your Should Know about the KBS Air Fryer Oven.

1. If you're cooking very fatty foods, add a little water to the drip pan below the basket tray to help prevent grease from getting too hot and smoking.
2. Don't overcrowd the mesh tray, but cook foods on one layer instead. I can't stress this enough. It's tempting to try to cook more at one time, but over-crowding will prevent foods from crisping and browning evenly and take more time over all.
3. Spray with oil part way through. If you are trying to get the food to brown and crisp more, try spritzing it with oil part way through the cooking process. This will also help the food to brown more evenly.
4. Place delicate items lower in the oven so they don't over brown or brown too quickly. Foods with ingredients like cheese or pastry on top can get too hot being too close to the upper element, so take advantage of the versatility of your air fryer oven and move the tray lower in the oven.
5. Always make sure the drip tray is underneath the mesh or perforated tray when you pull the tray out of the oven. Otherwise, grease and crumbs will drip or fall down on the oven door or countertop.
6. Don't pour away the juices from the drip tray too soon. The tray below the mesh basket tray collects a lot of juices from the cooked foods above and catches any marinades that you pour over the food. If the drippings are not too greasy, you can use this flavorful liquid as a sauce to pour over the food.

You can also de-grease this liquid and reduce it in a small saucepan on the stovetop for a few minutes to concentrate the flavor.

7. Wipe down the heating element and oven door after each use to prevent grease from building up inside your air fryer oven.
8. Use a bristle brush to clean the mesh racks or baskets in your air fryer after each use. Soaking the mesh basket in the drip tray while you enjoy dinner is enough to loosen any food stuck on the mesh.

Hints for Using Your KBS Air Fryer Oven

1. Always Preheat Before Cooking

Our first air fryer tip is to make sure you know how important it is to preheat the air fryer oven before cooking. Putting your food in a cold air fryer oven is similar to baking food in the oven without preheating it first. Not only will it throw the recipe cooking time off, but it won't evenly cook your food. Some air fryer oven models have a built in preheat button and others you'll just need to manually set and let the unit warm-up while you're prepping the recipe ingredients.

To preheat the air fryer, set the temperature to whatever the temperature of the recipe will be, and then let it heat for 3-5 minutes before adding the food.

2. Internet Recipes are a Guideline

Finding air fryer recipes on the internet is an easy and free way to have a constant source of recipes to try for the air fryer. Yet because makes and models can vary, it's good to keep a close eye on the food the first time you try a recipe.

For instance, with our first two air fryers, when we cooked wings, they were done exactly at 19 minutes. One was a small basket style air fryer and the other was a large air fryer toaster oven. Boy was I ever thrilled to see similar results!

But then when I purchased our latest (and actually favorite!) air fryer, I put the wings in for 19 minutes "like usual" and they were a little dry and overcooked.

The learning experience here and the air fryer tip for you is that the first time you make a recipe, keep a closer eye on it than usual and start checking the food for doneness a few min

3. Don't Overcrowd

You've probably seen the photos online of filled to the brim air fryers overflowing with french fries. And while that concept sure looks enticing, in reality, filling the air fryer prevents air circulation, makes it more difficult for food to cook evenly, plus some of the food doesn't turn out as crispy as it should.

4. Using the Air Fryer Oven to Reheat Foods

I'm sure after purchasing your air fryer oven you instantly thought of all of the amazing recipes you could make like wings, pork chops, and juicy chicken breasts. What might not have instantly come to mind was using the air fryer oven to reheat leftovers instead of reheating them in the microwave.

Do you have leftover onion rings from your favorite burger joint last night? Reheating them in a microwave will give you hot, yet soggy onion rings. If you use your air fryer instead, you'll end up with crispy rings that taste freshly cooked.

We even reheated leftover restaurant nachos recently by laying down some parchment paper in the basket and placing the nachos on top of that.

Most foods will take about 5 minutes to reheat on 400°F. This is one of those times we often skip preheating the unit since we're just trying to warm and re-crisp the food.

Better to Clean and Care for Your KBS Air Fryer Oven

Clean the Air Fryer Oven and its loose parts thoroughly after each use.

1. Press the on/off button and take the plug out of the socket.
2. Let the appliance cool down.
3. Take all the accessories from the appliance.
4. Remove remaining food parts by wiping them off with absorbent paper towels.
5. Clean the accessories thoroughly with hot water, dish-washing soap and a non-grating sponge.
6. The accessories can also be cleaned in a dish-washing machine. Dry them off thoroughly after cleaning.
7. Clean the housing and interior cavity with a moist towel, if need be with some dish-washing soap added to it. Dry it off thoroughly after cleaning.
8. Reassemble the parts.
9. Store the appliance in a dry place.

CAUTION:

- Verify that the appliance is not connected to the power supply before you clean it.
- Never use corrosive or scouring cleaning agents or sharp objects (such as knives or hard brushes) to clean the appliance.
- Never immerse the heating element unit in water or another liquid and never place it under flowing water.

BREAKFAST

Fry Bread

Servings: 4

Cooking Time: 5 Minutes

Ingredients:

- 1 cup flour
- 2 teaspoons baking powder
- ¼ teaspoon salt
- ¼ cup lukewarm milk
- 1 teaspoon oil
- 2–3 tablespoons water
- oil for misting or cooking spray

Directions:

1. Stir together flour, baking powder, and salt. Gently mix in the milk and oil. Stir in 1 tablespoon water. If needed, add more water 1 tablespoon at a time until stiff dough forms. Dough shouldn't be sticky, so use only as much as you need.
2. Divide dough into 4 portions and shape into balls. Cover with a towel and let rest for 10 minutes.
3. Preheat the toaster oven to 390°F.
4. Shape dough as desired:
5. a. Pat into 3-inch circles. This will make a thicker bread to eat plain or with a sprinkle of cinnamon or honey butter. You can cook all 4 at once.
6. b. Pat thinner into rectangles about 3 x 6 inches. This will create a thinner bread to serve as a base for dishes such as Indian tacos. The circular shape is more traditional, but rectangles allow you to cook 2 at a time in your air fryer oven.
7. Spray both sides of dough pieces with oil or cooking spray.
8. Place the 4 circles or 2 of the dough rectangles in the air fryer oven and air-fry at 390°F for 3 minutes. Spray tops, turn, spray other side, and air fry for 2 more minutes. If necessary, repeat to cook remaining bread.
9. Serve piping hot as is or allow to cool slightly and add toppings to create your own Native American tacos.

Country Bread

Servings: 2

Cooking Time: 30 Minutes

Ingredients:

- Yeast mixture:
- 1¼-ounce package active dry yeast
- ¼ cup skim milk, at room temperature
- 1 teaspoon brown sugar
- Flour mixture:
- ¾ cup tepid water
- 2½ cups unbleached flour
- 1 egg
- 2 teaspoons granulated sugar
- 2 tablespoons vegetable oil
- 2 tablespoons wheat germ
- Salt to taste
- Vegetable oil
- 1 egg, beaten, to brush the top

Directions:

1. Combine the yeast mixture ingredients in a large bowl and let stand for 10 minutes, or until the yeast is dissolved and foamy.

2. Add the flour mixture ingredients to the yeast mixture, blending well. Turn out the mixture on a lightly floured surface.
3. KNEAD the dough for 6 minutes, or until smooth and elastic. Return the dough to the large bowl, cover with a clean damp towel, and put in a warm place for 1 hour, or until doubled in size.
4. Punch down the dough and turn out onto a lightly floured surface. Knead for 2 minutes, then place the dough in an oiled or nonstick regular size 8½ × 4½ × 2¼-inch loaf pan. Brush the loaf with vegetable oil, cover the pan with a damp towel, and place in a warm place for 1 hour, or until doubled in size. Brush the loaf with the beaten egg.
5. Preheat the toaster oven to 375° F.
6. BAKE for 30 minutes, or until a toothpick inserted in the middle comes out clean and the top is browned. Sharply tap the pan to loosen the loaf, invert, and place on a rack to cool.

Ham, Egg, And Cheese Sandwiches

Servings: 4
Cooking Time: 60 Minutes

Ingredients:

- 8 large eggs
- ½ cup milk
- ½ teaspoon table salt
- 3 tablespoons mayonnaise
- 1 tablespoon Dijon mustard
- 4 slices deli ham
- 4 ounces Gruyère cheese, shredded (1 cup)
- 4 hamburger buns, toasted
- 1 ounce (1 cup) baby arugula

Directions:

1. Adjust toaster oven rack to middle position and preheat the toaster oven to 300 degrees. Generously spray bottom and sides of 8-inch square baking pan with vegetable oil spray. Whisk eggs, milk, and salt in bowl until well combined. Transfer egg mixture to prepared pan, cover tightly with aluminum foil, and bake until egg is set, 30 to 35 minutes, rotating pan halfway through baking.
2. Run thin knife between egg and side of pan. Invert egg onto cutting board and cut into four squares. Combine mayonnaise and mustard in small bowl. (Egg squares and mayonnaise-mustard mixture can be refrigerated separately for up to 3 days. To reheat egg squares, increase bake time in step 3 to 4 to 6 minutes.)
3. Arrange desired number of egg squares on greased small rimmed baking sheet and top each square with 1 slice ham and ¼ cup Gruyère. Bake until ham is heated through and Gruyère is melted, 2 to 4 minutes.
4. Spread 1 tablespoon mayonnaise-mustard mixture on each bun top. Place egg squares on bun bottoms and top each with ¼ cup arugula and bun tops. Serve.

Pancake Muffins

Servings: 4
Cooking Time: 8 Minutes

Ingredients:

- 1 cup flour
- 2 tablespoons sugar (optional)
- ½ teaspoon baking soda
- 1 teaspoon baking powder
- ¼ teaspoon salt
- 1 egg, beaten
- 1 cup buttermilk

- 2 tablespoons melted butter
- 1 teaspoon pure vanilla extract
- 24 foil muffin cups
- cooking spray
- Suggested Fillings
- 1 teaspoon of jelly or fruit preserves
- 1 tablespoon or less fresh blueberries; chopped fresh strawberries; chopped frozen cherries; dark chocolate chips; chopped walnuts, pecans, or other nuts; cooked, crumbled bacon or sausage

Directions:

1. In a large bowl, stir together flour, optional sugar, baking soda, baking powder, and salt.
2. In a small bowl, combine egg, buttermilk, butter, and vanilla. Mix well.
3. Pour egg mixture into dry ingredients and stir to mix well but don't overbeat.
4. Double up the muffin cups and remove the paper liners from the top cups. Spray the foil cups lightly with cooking spray.
5. Place 6 sets of muffin cups in air fryer oven. Pour just enough batter into each cup to cover the bottom. Sprinkle with desired filling. Pour in more batter to cover the filling and fill the cups about ¾ full.
6. Air-fry at 330°F for 8 minutes.
7. Repeat steps 5 and 6 for the remaining 6 pancake muffins.

Onion And Cheese Buttermilk Biscuits

Servings: 4

Cooking Time: 15 Minutes

Ingredients:

- 2 cups unbleached flour
- 3 tablespoons margarine, at room temperature
- ¾ cup low-fat buttermilk
- 4 teaspoons baking powder
- 1 teaspoon garlic powder
- ¼ cup grated Parmesan cheese
- 3 tablespoons finely chopped onion
- 2 tablespoons chopped fresh parsley
- Salt to taste

Directions:

1. Preheat the toaster oven to 400° F.
2. Blend all the ingredients in a medium bowl with a fork, then press together to form a dough ball.
3. KNEAD the dough on a lightly floured surface just until smooth.
4. Roll the dough to ½-inch thickness and cut with a round 3-inch cookie cutter. Place on an oiled or nonstick 6½ × 10-inch baking sheet or in an oiled or nonstick 8½ × 8½ × 2-inch square baking (cake) pan.
5. BAKE for 15 minutes, or until lightly browned.

Flaky Granola

Servings: 3

Cooking Time: 20 Minutes

Ingredients:

- ¼ cup rolled oats
- ½ cup wheat flakes
- ½ cup bran flakes
- ¼ cup wheat germ
- 3 tablespoons sesame seeds
- 4 ¼ cup unsweetened shredded coconut
- ½ cup chopped almonds, walnuts, or pecans
- 2 tablespoons chopped pumpkin seeds
- ½ cup honey or molasses
- 2 tablespoons vegetable oil
- Salt to taste

Directions:

1. Preheat the toaster oven to 375° F.
2. Combine all the ingredients in a medium bowl, stirring to mix well.
3. Spread the mixture in an oiled or nonstick 6½ × 6½ × 2-inch square (cake) pan.
4. BAKE for 20 minutes, turning with tongs every 5 minutes to toast evenly. Cool and store in an airtight container in the refrigerator.

Turkey Burgers

Servings: 4
Cooking Time: 24 Minutes

Ingredients:

- 1 pound lean ground turkey breast
- 2 tablespoons bread crumbs
- 3 2 tablespoons barbecue sauce
- 4 ½ teaspoon garlic powder
- ½ teaspoon chili powder
- Salt and freshly ground black pepper to taste

Directions:

1. Combine all ingredients in a bowl, mixing well. Divide into 4 portions and shape into patties.
2. BROIL on a rack with a pan underneath for 20 minutes, or until the meat is browned and the juice runs clear when pierced with a fork.

Homemade Biscuits

Servings: 12
Cooking Time: 28 Minutes

Ingredients:

- 1 1/2 cups milk
- 1 tablespoon white vinegar
- 4 cups all-purpose flour
- 1/4 cup sugar
- 1 tablespoon plus 1 1/2 teaspoons baking powder
- 1 teaspoon salt
- 1 cup unsalted butter, cut into pieces
- Sausage Gravy

Directions:

1. Preheat the toaster oven to 375°F. Line a cookie sheet with parchment paper.
2. In a small bowl, stir milk and vinegar until blended. Set aside.
3. In a large bowl, combine flour, sugar, baking powder and salt. Cut in butter with a fork or a pastry blender until coarse crumbs form. Stir in the milk mixture until moistened (dough will be slightly moist).
4. On a well floured surface, roll dough to 3/4-inch thickness. Cut with a 3-inch round cookie cutter and arrange 2-inches apart on cookie sheet. Repeat with remaining dough.
5. Bake 26 to 28 minutes or until lightly browned.
6. Serve with Sausage Gravy, if desired.

Savory Breakfast Bread Pudding

Servings: 4
Cooking Time: 30 Minutes

Ingredients:

- Oil spray (hand-pumped)
- 4 slices whole-wheat bread, cubed
- 1 cup frozen potato hash browns, thawed
- 5 large eggs
- 1 cup whole milk
- ½ cup diced ham
- ½ cup shredded cheddar cheese
- 1 teaspoon fresh parsley, chopped
- ⅛ teaspoon sea salt
- ⅛ teaspoon freshly ground black pepper

Directions:

1. Place the baking tray on position 1 and preheat the toaster oven on BAKE to 350°F for 5 minutes.
2. Lightly oil an 8-inch-square baking dish with spray.
3. Spread the bread cubes and potatoes in the baking dish evenly.
4. In a medium bowl, combine the eggs, milk, ham, cheese, parsley, salt, and pepper.
5. Pour the egg mixture over the bread and potatoes in the dish.
6. Bake for 30 minutes. The bread pudding should be lightly golden, the eggs set, and a knife inserted in the center should come out clean.
7. Cool the pudding for 5 minutes and serve.

Garlic-cheese Biscuits

Servings: 8

Cooking Time: 8 Minutes

Ingredients:

- 1 cup self-rising flour
- 1 teaspoon garlic powder
- 2 tablespoons butter, diced
- 2 ounces sharp Cheddar cheese, grated
- ½ cup milk
- cooking spray

Directions:

1. Preheat the toaster oven to 330°F.
2. Combine flour and garlic in a medium bowl and stir together.
3. Using a pastry blender or knives, cut butter into dry ingredients.
4. Stir in cheese.
5. Add milk and stir until stiff dough forms.
6. If dough is too sticky to handle, stir in 1 or 2 more tablespoons of self-rising flour before shaping. Biscuits should be firm enough to hold their shape. Otherwise, they'll stick to the air fryer oven.
7. Divide dough into 8 portions and shape into 2-inch biscuits about ¾-inch thick.
8. Spray air fryer oven with nonstick cooking spray.
9. Place all 8 biscuits in air fryer oven and air-fry at 330°F for 8 minutes.

Sam's Maple Raisin Bran Muffins

Servings: 12

Cooking Time: 15 Minutes

Ingredients:

- 2 cups oat bran
- 2 teaspoons baking powder
- 2 eggs
- 1¼ cups low-fat soy milk
- ¾ cup raisins
- 3 tablespoons maple syrup
- 2 tablespoons vegetable oil
- Pinch of salt (optional)

Directions:

1. Preheat toaster oven to 425° F.
2. Combine all the ingredients in a bowl and stir until well blended. In a six-muffin 7 × 10 × 1½-inch tin, brush the pans with vegetable oil or use baking cups. Fill the pans or cups three-fourths full with batter.
3. BAKE for 15 minutes, or until a toothpick inserted in the center of a muffin comes out clean.

Buttered Poppy Seed Bread

Servings: 6

Cooking Time: 25 Minutes

Ingredients:

- 3 tablespoons unsalted butter, melted
- 1 (1-pound) loaf frozen white bread dough

- 1 teaspoon poppy seeds
- ¼ teaspoon onion powder
- ¼ teaspoon garlic powder
- ¼ teaspoon freshly ground black pepper

Directions:

1. Pour about half of the melted butter into a 9 x 5-inch loaf pan. Brush the butter to cover the sides and bottom of the pan. Place the frozen bread loaf in the pan. Brush the top of the loaf with the remaining butter, covering completely. Stir the poppy seeds, onion powder, garlic powder, and pepper in a small bowl. Sprinkle the seasonings over the top of the bread. Cover with plastic wrap and refrigerate overnight.
2. Remove the bread from the refrigerator and loosen the plastic wrap so it is loosely covered. Let it rise at room temperature until the top of the bread is just over the top edge of the pan, about 2 to 4 hours.
3. Preheat the toaster oven to 350°F.
4. Bake for 20 to 25 minutes or until the bread is golden brown.
5. Let cool for 5 minutes, then remove the loaf from the pan and place on a wire rack to cool for a few minutes. Slice and serve warm.

Almond Granola With Dried Fruit

Servings: 5

Cooking Time: 45 Minutes

Ingredients:

- 2½ tablespoons maple syrup
- 2½ tablespoons packed light brown sugar
- 2 teaspoons vanilla extract
- ¼ teaspoon table salt
- ¼ cup vegetable oil
- 2½ cups (7½ ounces) old-fashioned rolled oats
- 1 cup whole almonds, chopped
- 1 cup raisins, currants, dried cranberries, and/or chopped dried cherries

Directions:

1. Adjust toaster oven rack to middle position and preheat the toaster oven to 325 degrees. Line small rimmed baking sheet with parchment paper.
2. Whisk maple syrup, sugar, vanilla, and salt together in large bowl, then whisk in oil until fully combined. Fold in oats and almonds until thoroughly coated. Transfer oat mixture to prepared sheet and spread into even layer. Using stiff metal spatula, compress oat mixture until very compact. Bake until lightly browned, 35 to 45 minutes, rotating sheet halfway through baking.
3. Remove granola from oven and let cool on wire rack to room temperature, about 1 hour. Break cooled granola into pieces of desired size and transfer to large clean bowl. Add dried fruit and gently toss to combine. (Granola can be stored in airtight container for up to 2 weeks.)

Baked Eggs With Bacon-tomato Sauce

Servings: 1

Cooking Time: 12 Minutes

Ingredients:

- 1 teaspoon olive oil
- 2 tablespoons finely chopped onion
- 1 teaspoon chopped fresh oregano
- pinch crushed red pepper flakes
- 1 (14-ounce) can crushed or diced tomatoes
- salt and freshly ground black pepper
- 2 slices of bacon, chopped

- 2 large eggs
- ¼ cup grated Cheddar cheese
- fresh parsley, chopped

Directions:

1. Start by making the tomato sauce. Preheat a medium saucepan over medium heat on the stovetop. Add the olive oil and sauté the onion, oregano and pepper flakes for 5 minutes. Add the tomatoes and bring to a simmer. Season with salt and freshly ground black pepper and simmer for 10 minutes.
2. Meanwhile, preheat the toaster oven to 400°F and pour a little water into the bottom of the air fryer oven. (This will help prevent the grease that drips into the bottom drawer from burning and smoking.) Place the bacon in the air fryer oven and air-fry at 400°F for 5 minutes.
3. When the bacon is almost crispy, remove it to a paper-towel lined plate and rinse out the air fryer oven, draining away the bacon grease.
4. Transfer the tomato sauce to a shallow 7-inch pie dish. Crack the eggs on top of the sauce and scatter the cooked bacon back on top. Season with salt and freshly ground black pepper and transfer the pie dish into the air fryer oven. You can use an aluminum foil sling to help with this by taking a long piece of aluminum foil, folding it in half lengthwise twice until it is roughly 26-inches by 3-inches. Place this under the pie dish and hold the ends of the foil to move the pie dish in and out of the air fryer oven. Tuck the ends of the foil beside the pie dish while it cooks in the air fryer oven.
5. Air-fry at 400°F for 5 minutes, or until the eggs are almost cooked to your liking. Sprinkle cheese on top and air-fry for an additional 2 minutes. When the cheese has melted, remove the pie dish from the air fryer oven, sprinkle with a little chopped parsley and let the eggs cool for a few minutes – just enough time to toast some buttered bread in your air fryer oven!

Bagel Melt

Servings: 1

Cooking Time: 3 Minutes

Ingredients:

- 1 bagel, split
- 4 slices Swiss cheese
- 4 strips lean turkey bacon, cut in half

Directions:

1. Layer the bagel halves with 2 slices of Swiss cheese and 4 half strips of turkey bacon each.
2. TOAST once on the oven rack.

Chocolate Chip Banana Muffins

Servings: 12

Cooking Time: 14 Minutes

Ingredients:

- 2 medium bananas, mashed
- ¼ cup brown sugar
- 1½ teaspoons vanilla extract
- ⅔ cup milk
- 2 tablespoons butter
- 1 large egg
- 1 cup white whole-wheat flour
- ½ cup old-fashioned oats
- 1 teaspoon baking soda
- ½ teaspoon baking powder
- ⅛ teaspoon sea salt
- ¼ cup mini chocolate chips

Directions:

1. Preheat the toaster oven to 330°F.

2. In a large bowl, combine the bananas, brown sugar, vanilla extract, milk, butter, and egg; set aside.
3. In a separate bowl, combine the flour, oats, baking soda, baking powder, and salt.
4. Slowly add the dry ingredients into the wet ingredients, folding in the flour mixture ⅓ cup at a time.
5. Mix in the chocolate chips and set aside.
6. Using silicone muffin liners, fill 6 muffin liners two-thirds full. Carefully place the muffin liners in the air fryer oven and bake for 20 minutes (or until the tops are browned and a toothpick inserted in the center comes out clean). Carefully remove the muffins from the air fryer oven and repeat with the remaining batter.
7. Serve warm.

Cinnamon Toast

Servings: 2
Cooking Time: 2 Minutes

Ingredients:

- 1 tablespoon brown sugar
- 2 teaspoons margarine, at room temperature
- ¼ teaspoon ground cinnamon
- 2 slices whole wheat or multigrain bread

Directions:

1. Combine the sugar, margarine, and cinnamon in a small bowl with a fork until well blended. Spread each bread slice with equal portions of the mixture.
2. TOAST once, or until the sugar is melted and the bread is browned to your preference.

Sun-dried Tomato Spread

Servings: 1
Cooking Time: 4 Minutes

Ingredients:

- ½ cup minced sun-dried tomatoes
- 3 tablespoons olive oil
- 2 tablespoons grated Parmesan cheese
- 1 teaspoon dried oregano or
- 1 tablespoon chopped fresh oregano
- 3 tablespoons chopped pecans or walnuts
- 2 garlic cloves, chopped
- Salt and freshly ground black pepper to taste

Directions:

1. Combine the sun-dried tomatoes and ⅔ cup water in an oiled or nonstick 8½ × 8½ × 2-inch baking (cake) pan.
2. BROIL for 4 minutes, or until the tomatoes are softened. Remove from the oven and transfer the tomatoes with the liquid to a bowl. Add all the other ingredients and mix well.
3. Process the mixture in a blender or food processor until smooth. Adjust the seasonings.

Yogurt Bread

Servings: 2
Cooking Time: 40 Minutes

Ingredients:

- 3 cups unbleached flour
- 4 teaspoons baking powder
- 5 2 teaspoons sugar
- Salt to taste
- 1 cup plain nonfat yogurt
- ¼ cup vegetable oil
- 1 egg, beaten, to brush the top

Directions:

1. Preheat the toaster oven to 375° F.
2. Combine the flour, baking powder, sugar, and salt in a large bowl. Make a hole in the center and spoon in the yogurt and oil.

3. Stir the flour into the center. When the dough is well mixed, turn it out onto a lightly floured surface and knead for 8 minutes, until the dough is smooth and elastic. Place the dough in an oiled or nonstick regular-size 8½ × 4½ × 2¼-inch loaf pan. Brush the top with the beaten egg.
4. BAKE for 40 minutes, or until a toothpick inserted in the center comes out clean and the loaf is browned. Invert on a wire rack to cool.

Cinnamon Swirl Bread

Servings: 4
Cooking Time: 50 Minutes

Ingredients:

- 2 cups all-purpose flour
- 1 cup granulated sugar
- 1 teaspoon baking soda
- ½ teaspoon table salt
- 1 teaspoon cider vinegar
- 1 cup whole milk
- 1 large egg
- ¼ cup canola or vegetable oil
- FILLING
- ½ cup granulated sugar
- 1 tablespoon ground cinnamon
- GLAZE
- ¼ cup confectioners' sugar
- 2 teaspoons whole milk

Directions:

1. Preheat the toaster oven to 350 °F. Grease the bottom of a 9 x 5-inch loaf pan.
2. Combine the flour, granulated sugar, baking soda, and salt in a large bowl. Place the vinegar in a 1-cup liquid measuring cup and add the milk; stir to combine. Whisk the milk mixture, egg, and oil in a medium bowl. Stir into the flour mixture, blending until combined.
3. Make the filling: Combine the granulated sugar and cinnamon in a small bowl.
4. Pour half of the batter into the prepared pan. Sprinkle half the cinnamon-sugar mixture over the batter in the loaf pan. Top with the remaining batter and sprinkle with remaining cinnamon-sugar mixture. Using a butter knife, make deep swirls in the batter. Make sure most of the cinnamon-sugar mixture from the top is covered in batter.
5. Bake for 45 to 50 minutes, or until a wooden pick inserted into the center comes out clean. Cool on a wire rack for 10 minutes. Run a knife around the edges of the bread, then remove the bread from the pan. Cool for an additional 10 minutes.
6. Meanwhile, make the glaze: Whisk the confectioners' sugar and milk in a small bowl until smooth. Drizzle the glaze over the partially cooled loaf. Serve warm or at room temperature.

Garlic Cheese Pull-apart Bread

Servings: 6
Cooking Time: 26 Minutes

Ingredients:

- 1 (1-pound) loaf frozen white bread dough
- Canola or vegetable oil
- Nonstick cooking spray
- 6 tablespoons unsalted butter, melted
- 3 cloves garlic, finely minced
- 2 tablespoons minced fresh flat-leaf (Italian) parsley
- ¼ teaspoon table salt
- ¼ teaspoon freshly ground black pepper
- ⅔ cup shredded Parmesan cheese
- ¾ cup shredded mozzarella cheese

Directions:

1. Rub the frozen dough lightly with the oil. Place it in a zip-top bag and refrigerate overnight to thaw.
2. Spray a 9 x 5-inch loaf pan with nonstick cooking spray.
3. Stir the butter, garlic, parsley, salt, and pepper in a small bowl; set aside.
4. Place the thawed dough on a lightly floured board and roll into a 12-inch square. Brush about 3 tablespoons of the butter mixture over the top of the dough. Sprinkle evenly with about ½ cup Parmesan and ½ cup mozzarella. Roll the dough over the filling, jelly-roll style. Cut into rolls ½ to ¾ inch thick. Stand the rolls upright in the loaf pan, two across, with the cut side of the rolls facing the narrow end of the pan. (There will be two rows, side by side, with 8 to 10 rolls in each row.) Cover with a towel and let rise for about 1 hour.
5. Preheat the toaster oven to 350°F. Bake for 18 to 23 minutes, or until the loaf is golden brown. Drizzle with the remaining melted butter mixture. Sprinkle with the remaining 2 tablespoons Parmesan cheese and the remaining¼ cup mozzarella cheese. Bake for 2 to 3 minutes for the cheese to melt.
6. Place the pan on a wire rack and let stand for 5 minutes. Remove the loaf from the pan. Serve warm.

Zucchini Bread

Servings: 6
Cooking Time: 30 Minutes

Ingredients:

- 1 cup grated zucchini
- 2 tablespoons grated onion
- 2 tablespoons grated Parmesan Cheese
- ½ cup skim milk
- 1 egg
- 2 tablespoons vegetable oil
- 1½ cups unbleached flour
- 1 tablespoon baking powder
- Salt to taste

Directions:

1. Preheat the toaster oven to 375° F.
2. Stir together all the ingredients in a medium bowl until smooth. Pour the batter into an oiled or nonstick regular-size 8½ × 4½ × 2¼-inch loaf pan.
3. BAKE for 30 minutes, or until a toothpick inserted in the center comes out clean.

Not-so-english Muffins

Servings: 4
Cooking Time: 10 Minutes

Ingredients:

- 2 strips turkey bacon, cut in half crosswise
- 2 whole-grain English muffins, split
- 1 cup fresh baby spinach, long stems removed
- ¼ ripe pear, peeled and thinly sliced
- 4 slices Provolone cheese

Directions:

1. Place bacon strips in air fryer oven and air-fry for 2minutes. Check and separate strips if necessary so they cook evenly. Air-fry for 4 more minutes, until crispy. Remove and drain on paper towels.
2. Place split muffin halves in air fryer oven and air-fry at 390°F for 2minutes, just until lightly browned.
3. Open air fryer oven and top each muffin with a quarter of the baby spinach, several pear slices, a strip of bacon, and a slice of cheese.
4. Air-fry at 360°F for 2minutes, until cheese completely melts.

Cinnamon Biscuit Rolls

Servings: 12
Cooking Time: 5 Minutes

Ingredients:

- Dough
- ¼ cup warm water (105–115°F)
- 1 teaspoon active dry yeast
- 1 tablespoon sugar
- ½ cup buttermilk, lukewarm
- 2 cups flour, plus more for dusting
- 1 teaspoon baking powder
- ½ teaspoon salt
- 3 tablespoons cold butter
- Filling
- 1 tablespoon butter, melted
- 1 teaspoon cinnamon
- 2 tablespoons sugar
- Icing
- ⅔ cup powdered sugar
- ¼ teaspoon vanilla
- 2–3 teaspoons milk

Directions:

1. Dissolve yeast and sugar in warm water. Add buttermilk, stir, and set aside.
2. In a large bowl, sift together flour, baking powder, and salt. Using knives or a pastry blender, cut in butter until mixture is well combined and crumbly.
3. Pour in buttermilk mixture and stir with fork until a ball of dough forms.
4. Knead dough on a lightly floured surface for 5 minutes. Roll into an 8 x 11-inch rectangle.
5. For the filling, spread the melted butter over the dough.
6. In a small bowl, stir together the cinnamon and sugar, then sprinkle over dough.
7. Starting on a long side, roll up dough so that you have a roll about 11 inches long. Cut into 12 slices with a serrated knife and sawing motion so slices remain round.
8. Place rolls on a plate or cookie sheet about an inch apart and let rise for 30 minutes.
9. For icing, mix the powdered sugar, vanilla, and milk. Stir and add additional milk until icing reaches a good spreading consistency.
10. Preheat the toaster oven to 360°F.
11. Place 6 cinnamon rolls in baking pan and cook 5 minutes or until top springs back when lightly touched. Repeat to cook remaining 6 rolls.
12. Spread icing over warm rolls and serve.

Walnut Pancake

Servings: 4
Cooking Time: 20 Minutes

Ingredients:

- 3 tablespoons butter, divided into thirds
- 1 cup flour
- 1½ teaspoons baking powder
- ¼ teaspoon salt
- 2 tablespoons sugar
- ¾ cup milk
- 1 egg, beaten
- 1 teaspoon pure vanilla extract
- ½ cup walnuts, roughly chopped
- maple syrup or fresh sliced fruit, for serving

Directions:

1. Place 1 tablespoon of the butter in air fryer oven baking pan. Air-fry at 330°F for 3 minutes to melt.
2. In a small dish or pan, melt the remaining 2 tablespoons of butter either in the microwave or on the stove.

3. In a medium bowl, stir together the flour, baking powder, salt, and sugar. Add milk, beaten egg, the 2 tablespoons of melted butter, and vanilla. Stir until combined but do not beat. Batter may be slightly lumpy.
4. Pour batter over the melted butter in air fryer oven baking pan. Sprinkle nuts evenly over top.
5. Air-fry for 20 minutes or until toothpick inserted in center comes out clean. Turn air fryer oven off, close the machine, and let pancake rest for 2 minutes.
6. Remove pancake from pan, slice, and serve with syrup or fresh fruit.

Apple Fritters

Servings: 6
Cooking Time: 12 Minutes

Ingredients:

- 1 cup all-purpose flour
- 1½ teaspoons baking powder
- ¼ teaspoon salt
- 2 tablespoon brown sugar
- 1 teaspoon vanilla extract
- ¾ cup plain Greek yogurt
- 1 tablespoon cinnamon
- 1 large Granny Smith apple, cored, peeled, and finely chopped
- ¼ cup chopped walnuts
- ½ cup powdered sugar
- 1 tablespoon milk

Directions:

1. Preheat the toaster oven to 320°F.
2. In a medium bowl, combine the flour, baking powder, and salt.
3. In a large bowl, add the brown sugar, vanilla, yogurt, cinnamon, apples, and walnuts. Mix the dry ingredients into the wet, using your hands to combine, until all the ingredients are mixed together. Knead the mixture in the bowl about 4 times.
4. Lightly spray the air fryer oven with olive oil spray.
5. Divide the batter into 6 equally sized balls; then lightly flatten them and place inside the air fryer oven. Repeat until all the fritters are formed.
6. Place in the air fryer oven and air-fry for 6 minutes, flip, and then cook another 6 minutes.
7. While the fritters are cooking, in a small bowl, mix the powdered sugar with the milk. Set aside.
8. When the cooking completes, remove the air fryer oven and allow the fritters to cool on a wire rack. Drizzle with the homemade glaze and serve.

Paleo Spiced Zucchini Bread

Servings: 8
Cooking Time: 45 Minutes

Ingredients:

- Dry Ingredients
- 1½ cups almond flour
- 2 tablespoons coconut flour
- 1 teaspoon cinnamon
- ¼ teaspoon allspice
- ⅛ teaspoon ground cloves
- 1 teaspoon baking powder
- ½ teaspoon baking soda
- ¼ teaspoon salt
- 1 cup chopped walnuts
- Wet Ingredients
- ⅓ cup coconut sugar
- 1 teaspoon vanilla extract
- 3 large eggs
- 5 tablespoons olive oil
- 2 tablespoons applesauce

- 1 cup shredded zucchini, squeezed to remove excess moisture

Directions:

1. Stir together all the dry ingredients in a large bowl.
2. Whisk all the wet ingredients in a separate bowl.
3. Add the dry ingredients to the wet ingredients and stir to combine. Allow the batter to rest for 5 minutes. This allows the coconut flour to absorb the batter.
4. Preheat the toaster Oven to 350°F.
5. Grease the mini loaf pans with coconut oil spray. Divide the batter evenly between the pans.
6. Place the mini loaf pans on the wire rack, then insert the rack at mid position in the preheated oven.
7. Select the Bake function, adjust time to 45 minutes, and press Start/Pause.
8. Remove when a toothpick or cake tester inserted into the middle comes out clean.
9. Remove zucchini bread from the pans and place on a cooling rack for 15 minutes before slicing.

Yogurt Cheese Spread

Servings: 1

Cooking Time: 5 Minutes

Ingredients:

- 1 cup plain yogurt (without starch, gum, or gelatin added)
- Seasonings:
- 1 tablespoon olive oil
- 1 teaspoon chopped fresh chives
- Salt and butcher's pepper or freshly ground black pepper to taste

Directions:

1. Place 2 coffee filters in a sieve over a bowl. Spoon the yogurt into the filters and place in the refrigerator for 6 to 8 hours, or until most of the moisture is drained from the yogurt and it is firm. Changing coffee filters several times during draining will expedite the process. Transfer the yogurt cheese to a bowl and add the oil, chives, and seasonings. Blend well and adjust the seasonings to taste.

LUNCH AND DINNER

Baked Parsleyed Cheese Grits

Servings: 4
Cooking Time: 30 Minutes

Ingredients:

- 4 strips lean uncooked turkey bacon, cut in half
- 1 cup grits
- 2 cups skim or low-fat soy milk
- 1 egg
- ½ cup shredded Parmesan cheese
- 1 tablespoon chopped fresh parsley
- ½ teaspoon garlic powder
- Salt and butcher's pepper to taste

Directions:

1. Preheat the toaster oven to 350° F.
2. Layer an 8½ × 8½ × 2-inch square baking (cake) pan with the bacon strips.
3. Combine the remaining ingredients in a medium bowl and pour the mixture over the strips.
4. BAKE, uncovered, for 30 minutes, or until the grits are cooked. Cut into squares with a spatula and serve.

Moussaka

Servings: 6
Cooking Time: 50 Minutes

Ingredients:

- 2 cups eggplant, peeled and cut into 1-inch cubes
- Beef mixture:
- 1 pound very lean ground beef
- 2 tablespoons finely chopped onion
- 3 4 tablespoons tomato paste
- ¼ cup dry red wine
- 2 tablespoons finely chopped fresh parsley
- ¼ teaspoon ground cinnamon
- Salt and freshly ground black pepper to taste
- Cheese mixture:
- 2 eggs, beaten
- 1 tablespoon unbleached flour
- ½ cup fat-free half-and-half
- ¼ teaspoon grated nutmeg
- 1 cup low-fat ricotta cheese
- Bread crumb mixture:
- 1 cup multigrain bread crumbs
- 1 cup freshly grated Parmesan cheese
- Olive oil

Directions:

1. Preheat the toaster oven to 375° F.
2. Dissolve 1 tablespoon salt in 2 cups water. Add the eggplant cubes and let soak for 10 minutes. Rinse well, drain, and pat with paper towel to remove any excess moisture. Set aside.
3. Combine the beef mixture ingredients in a medium bowl and set aside.
4. Whisk together the cheese mixture ingredients in a medium bowl and set aside.
5. Combine the bread crumb mixture in a medium bowl and set aside.
6. Layer half the eggplant cubes in a 1-quart 8½ × 8½ × 4-inch ovenproof baking dish that has been brushed with olive oil.
7. Sprinkle the eggplant with half the bread crumb mixture.
8. Add a layer of half the beef mixture. Repeat the layering process, using up the remaining eggplant, beef, and bread crumb mixtures.
9. Pour the cheese mixture over the top.
10. BAKE, uncovered, for 50 minutes, or until the eggplant is tender and the top is golden.

Baked Picnic Pinto Beans

Servings: 4
Cooking Time: 40 Minutes

Ingredients:

- 1 tomato, peeled and finely chopped
- 2 15-ounce cans pinto beans, drained
- 6 lean turkey bacon strips, cooked, drained, and crumbled
- 1 cup good-quality dark beer or ale
- 3 tablespoons finely chopped onion
- 1 tablespoon ketchup
- 2 tablespoons molasses
- 1 teaspoon Dijon mustard
- 1 teaspoon Worcestershire sauce
- 1 teaspoon garlic powder
- Salt and butcher's pepper to taste

Directions:

1. Preheat the toaster oven to 375° F.
2. Peel the tomato by immersing it in boiling water for 1 minute. Remove with tongs and when cool enough to handle, pull the skin away with a sharp paring knife. Chop and place in a 1-quart 8½ × 8½ × 4-inch ovenproof baking dish. Add all the other ingredients, stirring to mix well. Adjust the seasonings to taste. Cover with aluminum foil.
3. BAKE, covered, for 40 minutes.

Couscous-stuffed Poblano Peppers

Servings: 6
Cooking Time: 35 Minutes

Ingredients:

- 2 tablespoons olive oil
- ⅔ cup Israeli couscous
- 1 ¼ cups vegetable broth or water
- Kosher salt and freshly ground black pepper
- ½ medium onion, chopped
- 2 cloves garlic, minced
- 1 teaspoon dried oregano leaves
- ½ teaspoon ground cumin
- 1 (14.5-ounce) can fire-roasted diced tomatoes, with liquid
- Nonstick cooking spray
- 3 large poblano peppers, halved lengthwise, seeds and stem removed
- 1 ½ cups shredded Mexican blend, pepper Jack, or sharp cheddar cheese
- Optional toppings: minced fresh cilantro, sliced jalapeño peppers, diced tomatoes, sliced green onions (white and green portions)

Directions:

1. Heat 1 tablespoon oil in a medium saucepan over medium heat. Add the couscous and cook, stirring frequently, until golden brown, 2 to 3 minutes. Stir in the broth and season with salt and pepper. Cover, reduce the heat to a simmer, and cook, stirring occasionally, for about 10 minutes or until the liquid is absorbed. Remove from the heat and let stand, covered, for 5 minutes. Remove the cover, stir, and set aside to cool.
2. Heat the remaining 1 tablespoon oil in a small saucepan over medium heat. Add the onion, and cook, stirring frequently, for 3 to 5 minutes or until tender. Stir in the garlic and cook for 30 seconds. Stir in the oregano and cumin and season with salt and pepper. Stir in the tomatoes and simmer for 5 minutes.
3. Preheat the toaster oven to 400°F. Spray a 9-inch square baking pan with nonstick cooking spray. Spoon about one-third of the tomato mixture into the prepared pan. Arrange the peppers, cut side up, in the pan.

4. Stir 1 cup of the cheese into the couscous. Spoon the couscous mixture into the peppers, mounding slightly. Spoon the remaining tomato mixture over the peppers. Cover the pan and bake for 30 minutes.
5. Uncover the pan and sprinkle with the remaining cheese. Bake for 5 minutes or until the cheese is melted.
6. Top as desired with any of the various topping choices.

My Favorite Pizza

Servings: 4
Cooking Time: 30 Minutes

Ingredients:

- 1 9-inch ready-made pizza crust
- 1 8-ounce can tomato sauce
- 1 tablespoon olive oil
- 1 cup skinless, boneless chicken breast, cooked and cubed
- 3 plum tomatoes, chopped
- 1 bell pepper, quartered, seeded, and chopped
- 2 garlic cloves, minced
- ½ teaspoon dried oregano
- ½ teaspoon dried basil
- ½ teaspoon red pepper flakes
- 1 cup shredded part-skim, low-moisture mozzarella cheese

Directions:

1. Preheat the toaster oven to 400° F.
2. Spread the pizza crust with the tomato sauce. Drizzle with the olive oil and sprinkle with the chicken, tomatoes, pepper, garlic, seasonings, and cheese. Place the pizza on the toaster oven rack.
3. BAKE for 25 minutes, or until the topping is cooked and the crust is lightly browned.

Fillets En Casserole

Servings: 4
Cooking Time: 20 Minutes

Ingredients:

- ½ cup multigrain bread crumbs
- 4 6-ounce fish fillets
- Sauce:
- 2 tablespoons white wine
- 1 teaspoon Worcestershire sauce
- 1 teaspoon lemon juice
- 1 tablespoon vegetable oil
- 1 teaspoon Dijon mustard
- Salt and freshly ground black pepper to taste
- 2 tablespoons capers

Directions:

1. Preheat the toaster oven to 400° F.
2. Layer the bottom of an oiled or nonstick 8½ × 8½ × 2-inch square baking (cake) pan with the bread crumbs and place the fillets on the crumbs.
3. Combine the sauce ingredients, mixing well, and spoon over the fillets. Sprinkle with the capers.
4. BAKE, covered, for 20 minutes, or until the fish flakes easily with a fork.

Harvest Chicken And Rice Casserole

Servings: 4
Cooking Time: 42 Minutes

Ingredients:

- 4 skinless, boneless chicken thighs, cut into 1-inch cubes
- ½ cup brown rice 4 scallions, chopped
- 1 plum tomato, chopped
- 1 cup frozen peas
- 1 cup frozen corn

- 1 cup peeled and chopped carrots
- 2 tablespoons chopped fresh parsley
- 1 teaspoon mustard seed
- 1 teaspoon dried dill weed
- ¼ teaspoon celery seed
- Salt and freshly ground black pepper to taste
- ½ cup finely chopped pecans

Directions:

1. Preheat the toaster oven to 400° F.
2. Combine all the ingredients, except the pecans, with 2½ cups water in a 1-quart 8½ × 8½ × 4-inch ovenproof baking dish. Adjust the seasonings to taste. Cover with aluminum foil.
3. BAKE, covered, for 45 minutes, or until the rice is tender, stirring after 20 minutes to distribute the liquid. When done, uncover and sprinkle the top with the pecans.
4. BROIL for 7 minutes, or until the pecans are browned.

Inspirational Personal Pizza

Servings: 1

Cooking Time: 30 Minutes

Ingredients:

- 1 9-inch ready-made pizza crust
- 1 teaspoon olive oil
- 2 tablespoons tomato paste
- 4 ounces (½ cup) ground lean turkey breast
- 2 tablespoons sliced marinated artichokes
- 2 tablespoons pitted and chopped kalamata olives
- 2 tablespoons crumbled feta cheese
- 1 tablespoon chopped fresh basil leaves
- 1 tablespoon chopped fresh oregano leaves
- 2 tablespoons grated Parmesan cheese
- ¼ teaspoon red pepper flakes

Directions:

1. Preheat the toaster oven to 375°F.
2. Brush the pizza crust with the olive oil and spread on the tomato paste. Add all the other ingredients. Place the pizza on the toaster oven rack.
3. BAKE for 30 minutes, or until the topping is cooked and the crust is lightly browned.

Spanish Rice

Servings: 4

Cooking Time: 45 Minutes

Ingredients:

- ¾ cup rice
- 2 tablespoons dry white wine
- 3 tablespoons olive oil
- 1 15-ounce can whole tomatoes
- ¼ cup thinly sliced onions
- 3 tablespoons chopped fresh cilantro
- 4 ½ cup chopped bell pepper
- 5 2 bay leaves
- Salt and a pinch of red pepper flakes to taste

Directions:

1. Preheat the toaster oven to 375° F.
2. Combine all the ingredients with 1 cup water in a 1-quart 8½ × 8½ × 4-inch ovenproof baking dish and adjust the seasonings. Cover with aluminum foil.
3. BAKE, covered, for 45 minutes, or until the rice is cooked, removing the cover after 30 minutes.

Italian Stuffed Zucchini Boats

Servings: 6

Cooking Time: 26 Minutes

Ingredients:

- 6 small zucchini, halved lengthwise
- 1 pound bulk hot sausage

- 1 small onion, chopped
- 2 cloves garlic, minced
- 1 small Roma tomato, seeded and chopped
- 1/4 cup Parmesan cheese
- 3 tablespoons tomato paste
- 2 teaspoons dried Italian seasoning
- 1 teaspoon salt
- 1/2 teaspoon coarse black pepper
- 1 cup shredded mozzarella cheese
- Sliced fresh basil

Directions:

1. Preheat the toaster oven to 350°F. Spray a 13x9-inch baking pan with nonstick cooking spray.
2. Scoop out center of zucchini halves. Reserve 1 1/2 cups. Place zucchini boats in baking pan.
3. In a large skillet over medium-high heat, cook sausage, stirring to crumble, about 6 minutes or until browned. Remove sausage to a medium bowl.
4. Add onion and garlic to skillet, cook until onion is translucent. Stir in reserved zucchini, sausage, tomatoes, Parmesan cheese, tomato paste, Italian seasoning, salt and black pepper.
5. Spoon mixture into the zucchini boats.
6. Bake for 20 minutes. Remove from oven and top with mozzarella cheese.
7. Bake an additional 5 to 6 minutes or until cheese is melted.
8. Sprinkle with sliced fresh basil before serving.

Spanako Pizza

Servings: 2

Cooking Time: 30 Minutes

Ingredients:

- 8 sheets phyllo dough, thawed and folded in half
- 4 tablespoons olive oil
- 4 tablespoons grated Parmesan cheese
- Topping mixture:
- 1 10-ounce package frozen chopped spinach, thawed and well drained
- 1 plum tomato, finely chopped
- ¼ cup finely chopped onion
- ¼ cup shredded low-fat mozzarella cheese
- 3 tablespoons crumbled feta cheese or part-skim ricotta cheese
- 2 garlic cloves, minced
- Salt and freshly ground black pepper to taste

Directions:

1. Preheat the toaster oven to 375° F.
2. Layer the sheets of phyllo dough in an oiled or nonstick 9¾-inch-diameter baking pan, lightly brushing the top of each sheet with olive oil and folding in the corner edges to fit the pan.
3. Combine the topping mixture ingredients in a bowl and adjust the seasonings to taste. Spread the mixture on top of the phyllo pastry layers and sprinkle with the Parmesan cheese.
4. BAKE for 30 minutes, or until the cheese is melted and the topping is lightly browned. Remove carefully from the pan with a metal spatula.

Connecticut Garden Chowder

Servings: 4

Cooking Time: 60 Minutes

Ingredients:

- Soup:
- ½ cup peeled and shredded potato
- ½ cup shredded carrot
- ½ cup shredded celery 2 plum tomatoes, chopped
- 1 small zucchini, shredded

- 2 bay leaves
- ¼ teaspoon sage
- 1 teaspoon garlic powder
- Salt and butcher's pepper to taste
- Chowder base:
- 2 tablespoons reduced-fat cream cheese, at room temperature
- ½ cup fat-free half-and-half
- 2 tablespoons unbleached flour
- 2 tablespoons chopped fresh parsley

Directions:

1. Preheat the toaster oven to 375° F.
2. Combine the soup ingredients in a 1-quart 8½ × 8½ × 4-inch ovenproof baking dish, mixing well. Adjust the seasonings to taste.
3. BAKE, covered, for 40 minutes, or until the vegetables are tender.
4. Whisk the chowder mixture ingredients together until smooth. Add the mixture to the cooked soup ingredients and stir well to blend.
5. BAKE, uncovered for 20 minutes, or until the stock is thickened. Ladle the soup into individual soup bowls and garnish with the parsley.

Roasted Vegetable Gazpacho

Servings: 4

Cooking Time: 35 Minutes

Ingredients:

- Vegetables and seasonings:
- 1 bell pepper, thinly sliced
- ½ cup chopped celery
- ½ cup frozen or canned corn
- 1 medium onion, thinly sliced
- 1 small yellow squash, cut into 1-inch slices
- 1 small zucchini, cut into 1-inch slices
- 3 garlic cloves, chopped
- ½ teaspoon ground cumin
- 2 tablespoons olive oil
- Salt and freshly ground black pepper to taste
- 1 quart tomato juice
- 1 tablespoon lemon juice
- 3 tablespoons chopped fresh cilantro

Directions:

1. Preheat the toaster oven to 400°F.
2. Combine the vegetables and seasonings in an oiled or nonstick 8½ × 8½ × 2-inch square baking (cake) pan, mixing well.
3. BAKE, covered, for 25 minutes, or until the onions and celery are tender. Remove from the oven, uncover, and turn the vegetable pieces with tongs.
4. BROIL for 10 minutes, or until the vegetables are lightly browned. Remove from the oven and cool. Transfer to a large nonaluminum container and add the tomato juice, lemon juice, and cilantro. Adjust the seasonings.
5. Chill, covered, for several hours, preferably a day or two to enrich the flavor of the stock.

Baked Tomato Casserole

Servings: 4

Cooking Time:45 Minutes

Ingredients:

- Casserole mixture:
- 1 medium onion, coarsely chopped
- 3 medium tomatoes, coarsely chopped
- 1 medium green pepper, coarsely chopped
- 2 garlic cloves, minced
- ½ teaspoon crushed oregano
- ½ teaspoon crushed basil
- 1 tablespoon extra virgin olive oil
- 2 tablespoons chopped fresh cilantro
- Salt and freshly ground black pepper
- 3 4 tablespoons grated Parmesan cheese

- ¼ cup multigrain bread crumbs

Directions:

1. Preheat the toaster oven to 400° F.
2. Combine the casserole mixture ingredients in a 1-quart 8½ × 8½ × 4-inch ovenproof baking dish. Adjust the seasonings to taste and cover with aluminum foil.
3. BAKE, covered, for 35 minutes, or until the tomatoes and pepper are tender. Remove from the oven, uncover, and sprinkle with the bread crumbs and Parmesan cheese.
4. BROIL for 10 minutes, or until the topping is lightly browned.

Green Bean Soup

Servings: 4
Cooking Time: 47 Minutes

Ingredients:

- Roux mixture:
- 2 tablespoons unbleached flour
- 1 tablespoon margarine
- 3 cups water or low-sodium vegetable stock
- 1 cup (½ pound) fresh string beans, trimmed and cut into 1-inch pieces
- ½ teaspoon dried oregano
- ½ teaspoon ground cumin
- Salt and freshly ground black pepper to taste

Directions:

1. Combine the roux mixture in an 8½ × 8½ × 2-inch baking (cake) pan.
2. BROIL for 5 minutes, or until the margarine is melted. Remove from the oven and stir, then broil again for 2 minutes, or until the mixture is brown but not burned. Remove from the oven and stir to mix well. Set aside.
3. Combine the water or broth, string beans, and seasonings in a 1-quart 8½ × 8½ × 4-inch ovenproof baking dish. Stir in the roux mixture, blending well. Adjust the seasonings to taste.
4. BAKE, covered, at 375°F. for 40 minutes, or until the string beans are tender.

Salad Lentils

Servings: 4
Cooking Time: 35 Minutes

Ingredients:

- ¼ cup lentils
- 1 tablespoon olive oil
- Salad ingredients:
- 1 celery stalk, trimmed and Chopped
- 1 plum tomato, chopped
- 1 cucumber, peeled, seeded, and chopped
- 1½ cups spinach leaves, pulled into small pieces
- 1 tablespoon balsamic vinegar
- 1 tablespoon olive oil
- ½ teaspoon dried oregano
- 1 tablespoon chopped scallions
- 2 tablespoons sliced pitted black olives
- 1 teaspoon minced roasted garlic

Directions:

1. Preheat the toaster oven to 400° F.
2. Combine the lentils, ¼ cups water, and olive oil in a 1-quart 8½ × 8½ × 4-inch ovenproof baking dish. Cover with aluminum foil.
3. BAKE, covered, for 35 minutes, or until the lentils are tender. When cool, combine with all the salad ingredients in a serving bowl and toss well. Adjust the seasonings, chill, and serve.

Narragansett Clam Chowder

Servings: 4

Cooking Time: 35 Minutes

Ingredients:

- 1 cup fat-free half-and-half
- 2 tablespoons unbleached flour
- 3 ½ cup chopped onion
- 1 cup peeled and diced potato
- 1 tablespoon vegetable oil
- 1 tablespoon chopped fresh parsley
- 1 6-ounce can clams, drained and chopped
- 1 15-ounce can fat-free low-sodium chicken broth
- Salt and freshly ground black pepper

Directions:

1. Whisk together the half-and-half and flour in a small bowl. Set aside.
2. Combine the onion, potato, and oil in an 8½ × 8½ × 2-inch square baking (cake) pan.
3. BROIL 15 minutes, turning every 5 minutes with tongs, or until the potato is tender and the onion is cooked. Transfer to a 1-quart baking dish. Add the parsley, clams, broth, and half-and-half/flour mixture. Stir well and season to taste with salt and pepper.
4. BAKE, uncovered, at 375° F. for 20 minutes, stirring after 10 minutes, or until the stock is reduced and thickened. Ladle into bowls and serve with Yogurt Bread.

Zucchini Casserole

Servings: 4

Cooking Time: 37 Minutes

Ingredients:

- 4 small zucchini squashes, halved and quartered
- 2 plum tomatoes, quartered
- 1 8-ounce can tomato sauce
- 2 tablespoons chopped onion
- 2 garlic cloves, minced
- 1 tablespoon olive oil
- 1 tablespoon chopped fresh oregano
- 1 tablespoon chopped fresh basil
- 2 tablespoons pine nuts (pignoli)
- Salt and freshly ground black pepper to taste
- ½ cup shredded low-fat mozzarella cheese

Directions:

1. Preheat the toaster oven to 400° F.
2. Combine all the ingredients, except the mozzarella cheese, in a 1-quart 8½ × 8½ × 4-inch ovenproof baking dish. Cover with aluminum foil.
3. BAKE, covered, for 30 minutes, or until the zucchini is tender. Uncover and sprinkle the top with the cheese.
4. BROIL for 7 minutes, or until the cheese is melted and lightly browned.

Chicken Gumbo

Servings: 4

Cooking Time: 40 Minutes

Ingredients:

- 2 skinless, boneless chicken breast halves, cut into 1-inch cubes
- ½ cup dry red wine
- 1 small onion, finely chopped
- 1 celery stalk, finely chopped
- 2 plum tomatoes, chopped
- 3 1 bell pepper, chopped
- 1 tablespoon minced fresh garlic
- 2 okra pods, stemmed, seeded, and finely chopped 1 bay leaf
- ½ teaspoon hot sauce
- ½ teaspoon dried thyme

- Salt and freshly ground black pepper to taste

Directions:

1. Preheat the toaster oven to 400° F.
2. Combine all the ingredients in a 1-quart 8½ × 8½ × 4-inch ovenproof baking dish. Adjust the seasonings to taste. Cover with aluminum foil.
3. BAKE, covered, for 40 minutes, or until the onion, pepper, and celery are tender. Discard the bay leaf before serving.

One-step Classic Goulash

Servings: 4

Cooking Time: 56 Minutes

Ingredients:

- 1 cup elbow macaroni
- 1 cup (8-ounce can) tomato sauce
- 1 cup very lean ground round or sirloin
- 1 cup peeled and chopped fresh tomato
- ½ cup finely chopped onion
- 1 teaspoon garlic powder
- Salt and freshly ground black pepper
- Topping:
- 1 cup homemade bread crumbs
- 1 tablespoon margarine

Directions:

1. Preheat the toaster oven to 400° F.
2. Combine all the ingredients, except the topping, with 2 cups water in a 1-quart 8½ × 8½ × 4-inch ovenproof baking dish and mix well. Adjust the seasonings to taste. Cover with aluminum foil.
3. BAKE, covered, for 50 minutes, or until the macaroni is cooked, stirring after 25 minutes to distribute the liquid. Uncover, sprinkle with bread crumbs, and dot with margarine.
4. BROIL for 6 minutes, or until the topping is lightly browned.

Light Beef Stroganoff

Servings: 4

Cooking Time: 40 Minutes

Ingredients:

- Sauce:
- 1 cup skim milk
- 1 cup fat-free half-and-half
- 2 tablespoons reduced-fat cream cheese, at room temperature
- 4 tablespoons unbleached flour
- 2 pounds lean round or sirloin steak, cut into strips 2 inches long and ½ inch thick
- Browning mixture:
- 1 tablespoon soy sauce
- 2 tablespoons spicy brown mustard
- 1 tablespoon olive oil
- 2 teaspoons garlic powder
- Salt and freshly ground black pepper to taste

Directions:

1. Whisk together the sauce ingredients in a medium bowl until smooth. Set aside.
2. Combine the beef strips and browning mixture ingredients in an oiled or nonstick 8½ × 8½ × 2-inch square baking (cake) pan.
3. BROIL for 8 minutes, or until the strips are browned, turning with tongs after 4 minutes. Transfer to a 1-quart 8½ × 8½ × 4-inch ovenproof baking dish. Add the sauce and mix well. Adjust the seasonings to taste. Cover with aluminum foil.
4. BAKE, covered, for 40 minutes, or until the meat is tender.

Very Quick Pizza

Servings: 1
Cooking Time: 3 Minutes

Ingredients:

- 2 tablespoons salsa
- 1 6-inch whole wheat pita bread
- 2 tablespoons shredded part-skim, low-moisture mozzarella cheese

Directions:

1. Spread the salsa on the pita bread and sprinkle with the cheese.
2. TOAST once, or until the cheese is melted.

Fresh Herb Veggie Pizza

Servings: 4
Cooking Time: 25 Minutes

Ingredients:

- 1 9-inch ready-made pizza crust
- 1 tablespoon olive oil
- 1 4-ounce can tomato paste
- 2 tablespoons shredded part-skim mozzarella
- 2 tablespoons grated Parmesan cheese
- 2 tablespoons crumbled feta cheese
- ½ bell pepper, chopped
- 1 tablespoon chopped fresh parsley
- 1 tablespoon chopped fresh oregano
- 1 tablespoon chopped fresh basil
- ½ teaspoon red pepper flakes
- Salt and freshly ground black pepper to taste
- Pizza mixture:
- 2 garlic cloves, minced
- 1 plum tomato, chopped

Directions:

1. Preheat the toaster oven to 400° F.
2. Brush the pizza crust with olive oil and spread the tomato paste evenly to cover.
3. Combine the ingredients for the pizza mixture and spread evenly on top of the tomato paste layer. Sprinkle the cheeses over all and season to taste. Place the pizza on the toaster oven rack.
4. BAKE for 25 minutes, or until the vegetables are cooked and the cheese is melted.

Lima Bean And Artichoke Casserole

Servings: 4
Cooking Time: 40 Minutes

Ingredients:

- 1 15-ounce can lima beans, drained
- 1 6-ounce jar artichokes, marinated in olive oil (include the oil)
- ½ cup dry white wine
- 1 small onion, thinly sliced
- 2 medium carrots, thinly sliced
- 1 5-ounce can roasted peppers, drained and chopped
- ¼ teaspoon paprika
- ½ teaspoon ground cumin
- 1 teaspoon curry powder
- Salt and freshly ground black pepper to taste

Directions:

1. Preheat the toaster oven to 350° F.
2. Combine all the ingredients in a 1-quart 8½ × 8½ × 4-inch ovenproof baking dish, blending well. Adjust the seasonings to taste. Cover with aluminum foil.
3. BAKE, covered, for 40 minutes, or until the carrots and onion are tender.

Quick Pan Pizza

Servings: 8

Cooking Time: 22 Minutes

Ingredients:

- 1 can (13.8 oz.) refrigerator pizza crust, cut in half
- 2 tablespoons oil, divided
- 2/3 cup Slow Cooker Marinara Sauce, divided
- 2 cups shredded mozzarella cheese, divided
- 18 slices pepperoni, divided
- 1 small green pepper, sliced into rings, divided
- 2 large mushrooms, sliced, divided

Directions:

1. Preheat the toaster oven to 425°F. Spray baking pan with nonstick cooking spray.
2. Press half of dough into pan. Brush with 1 tablespoon oil.
3. Bake 8 to 9 minutes or until light brown.
4. Top baked crust with 1/3 cup sauce, 1 cup shredded mozzarella cheese and half of the pepperoni, green pepper and mushrooms.
5. Bake an additional 11 to 13 minutes or until cheese is melted and crust is brown. Repeat to make second pizza.

Pea Soup

Servings: 6

Cooking Time: 55 Minutes

Ingredients:

- 1 cup dried split peas, ground in a blender to a powderlike consistency
- 3 strips lean turkey bacon, uncooked and chopped
- ¼ cup grated carrots
- ¼ cup grated celery
- 2 tablespoons grated onion
- ½ teaspoon garlic powder
- Salt and freshly ground black pepper to taste
- Garnish:
- 2 tablespoons chopped fresh chives

Directions:

1. Preheat the toaster oven to 400° F.
2. Combine all the ingredients in a 1-quart 8½ × 8½ × 4-inch ovenproof baking dish, mixing well. Adjust the seasonings.
3. BAKE, covered, for 35 minutes. Remove from the oven and stir.
4. BAKE, covered, for another 20 minutes, or until the soup is thickened. Ladle the soup into individual soup bowls and garnish each with chopped fresh chives.

Italian Bread Pizza

Servings: 4

Cooking Time: 30 Minutes

Ingredients:

- 1 loaf Italian or French bread, unsliced
- Filling:
- ½ cup tomato sauce
- 2 tablespoons tomato paste
- 2 tablespoons olive oil
- ½ cup grated zucchini
- ½ cup grated onion
- 2 tablespoons grated bell pepper
- 1 teaspoon garlic powder
- 2 tablespoons chopped pitted black olives
- 1 teaspoon dried oregano or 1 tablespoon chopped fresh oregano
- Salt to taste
- ¼ cup mozzarella cheese

Directions:

1. Preheat the toaster oven to 375° F.

2. Cut the loaf of bread in half lengthwise, then in quarters crosswise. Remove some of the bread from the center to make a cavity for the pizza topping.
3. Combine all the topping ingredients and spoon equal portions into the cavities in the bread. Sprinkle with mozzarella cheese. Place the bread quarters on the toaster oven rack.
4. BAKE for 30 minutes, or until the cheese is melted and the crust is lightly browned.

Classic Beef Stew

Servings: 4
Cooking Time: 50 Minutes

Ingredients:

- 1½ cups dark beer
- 4 tablespoons unbleached flour
- 2 cups (approximately 1 pound) lean top round steak, cut into 1-inch cubes
- 1 cup peeled and coarsely chopped carrots
- 1 cup peeled and coarsely chopped potatoes
- ½ cup coarsely chopped onion
- 1 cup fresh or frozen peas
- 2 plum tomatoes, chopped
- 3 garlic cloves, minced
- 4 3 bay leaves
- ¼ teaspoon ground cumin
- Salt and butcher's pepper to taste

Directions:

1. Preheat the toaster oven to 400° F.
2. Whisk together the beer and flour in a 1-quart 8½ × 8½ × 4-inch ovenproof baking dish. Add all the other ingredients and seasonings and mix well, adjusting the seasonings to taste. Cover the dish with aluminum foil.
3. BAKE, covered, for 50 minutes, or until the meat is cooked and the vegetables are tender. Remove the bay leaves before serving.

SNACKS APPETIZERS AND SIDES

Loaded Potato Skins

Servings: 8

Cooking Time: 8 Minutes

Ingredients:

- 12 round baby potatoes
- 3 ounces cream cheese
- 4 slices cooked bacon, crumbled or chopped
- 2 green onions, finely chopped
- ½ cup grated cheddar cheese, divided
- ¼ cup sour cream
- 1 tablespoon milk
- 2 teaspoons hot sauce

Directions:

1. Preheat the toaster oven to 320°F.
2. Poke holes into the baby potatoes with a fork. Place the potatoes onto a microwave-safe plate and microwave on high for 4 to 5 minutes, or until soft to squeeze. Let the potatoes cool until they're safe to handle, about 5 minutes.
3. Meanwhile, in a medium bowl, mix together the cream cheese, bacon, green onions, and ¼ cup of the cheddar cheese; set aside.
4. Slice the baby potatoes in half. Using a spoon, scoop out the pulp, leaving enough pulp on the inside to retain the shape of the potato half. Place the potato pulp into the cream cheese mixture and mash together with a fork. Using a spoon, refill the potato halves with filling.
5. Place the potato halves into the air fryer oven and top with the remaining ¼ cup of cheddar cheese.
6. Cook the loaded baked potato bites in batches for 8 minutes.
7. Meanwhile, make the sour cream sauce. In a small bowl, whisk together the sour cream, milk, and hot sauce. Add more hot sauce if desired.
8. When the potatoes have all finished cooking, place them onto a serving platter and serve with sour cream sauce drizzled over the top or as a dip.

Bacon Corn Muffins

Servings: 6

Cooking Time: 17 Minutes

Ingredients:

- 1 1/4 cups self rising cornmeal mix
- 3/4 cup buttermilk
- 1/3 cup chopped cooked bacon
- 1/4 cup butter, melted
- 1 large egg, slightly beaten

Directions:

1. Preheat toaster oven to 425°F on CONVECTION setting.
2. Stir cornmeal mix, buttermilk, bacon, butter and egg until blended.
3. Spoon batter into lightly greased muffin pan, filling 3/4 full.
4. Bake 15 to 17 minutes until toothpick inserted in center comes out clean.
5. Cool 10 minutes on wire rack; remove.

Dill Fried Pickles With Light Ranch Dip

Servings: 4

Cooking Time: 8 Minutes

Ingredients:

- 4 to 6 large dill pickles, sliced in half or quartered lengthwise

- ½ cup all-purpose flour
- 2 eggs, lightly beaten
- 1 cup plain breadcrumbs
- 1 teaspoon salt
- ⅛ teaspoon cayenne pepper
- 2 tablespoons fresh dill leaves, dried well
- vegetable oil, in a spray bottle
- Light Ranch Dip
- ¼ cup reduced-fat mayonnaise
- ¼ cup buttermilk
- ¼ cup non-fat Greek yogurt
- 1 tablespoon chopped fresh chives
- 1 tablespoon chopped fresh parsley
- 1 tablespoon lemon juice
- salt and freshly ground black pepper

Directions:

1. Dry the dill pickle spears very well with a clean kitchen towel.
2. Set up a dredging station using three shallow dishes. Place the flour in the first shallow dish. Place the eggs into the second dish. Combine the breadcrumbs, salt, cayenne and fresh dill in a food processor and process until everything is combined and the crumbs are very fine. Place the crumb mixture in the third dish.
3. Preheat the toaster oven to 400°F.
4. Coat the pickles by dredging them first in the flour, then the egg, and then the breadcrumbs, pressing the crumbs on gently with your hands. Set the coated pickles on a tray and spray them on all sides with vegetable oil.
5. Air-fry one layer of pickles at a time at 400°F for 8 minutes, turning them over halfway through the cooking process and spraying lightly again if necessary. The crumbs should be nicely browned on all sides.
6. While the pickles are air-frying, make the light ranch dip by mixing everything together in a bowl. Serve the pickles warm with the dip on the side.

Sesame Green Beans

Servings: 4

Cooking Time: 8 Minutes

Ingredients:

- 1 pound green beans, stems trimmed
- 1 tablespoon olive oil
- 1 teaspoon sesame oil
- 1 tablespoon sesame seeds
- Pinch sea salt

Directions:

1. Preheat the toaster oven to 350°F on AIR FRY for 5 minutes.
2. In a large bowl, toss the green beans, olive oil, and sesame oil.
3. Place the air-fryer basket in the baking tray and spread the beans in the basket.
4. Place the tray in position 2 and air fry for 8 minutes, shaking the basket at the halfway point. The beans should be lightly golden and fragrant.
5. Transfer the beans to a serving plate and serve topped with the sesame seeds and seasoned with salt.

Roasted Brussels Sprouts Au Gratin

Servings: 6

Cooking Time: 36 Minutes

Ingredients:

- 1 pound fresh Brussels sprouts, trimmed and halved
- 2 tablespoons olive oil

- Kosher salt and freshly ground black pepper
- Nonstick cooking spray
- 2 slices bacon, cooked until crisp and crumbled
- 3 tablespoons unsalted butter
- 2 tablespoons all-purpose flour
- 1 cup whole milk
- 1 cup shredded Gruyère or Swiss cheese
- ½ teaspoon dried thyme leaves
- ¼ cup panko bread crumbs
- ¼ cup shredded Parmesan cheese

Directions:

1. Preheat the toaster oven to 450°F.
2. Toss the Brussels sprouts with the olive oil in a large bowl. Season with salt and pepper. Arrange the Brussels sprouts in a single layer in a 12 x 12-inch baking pan. Bake uncovered for 10 minutes. Stir and bake for an additional 8 to 10 minutes, or until the edges are beginning to char and the Brussels sprouts are just tender. Remove from the oven.
3. Reduce the toaster oven to 375°F. Spray a 1 ½-quart casserole dish or an 8 x 8-inch square baking pan with nonstick cooking spray. Place the Brussels sprouts in the casserole dish. Sprinkle with the crisp bacon.
4. Melt 2 tablespoons of the butter in a small saucepan over medium heat. Stir in the flour, blending until smooth and cook, stirring constantly, for 1 minute. Gradually add the milk and cook, stirring constantly, until the mixture is bubbly and thickened. Season with salt and pepper. Stir in the cheese and thyme and cook, stirring until melted. Pour the sauce over the Brussels sprouts.
5. Melt the remaining tablespoon of butter. Stir in the panko bread crumbs and Parmesan cheese. Sprinkle the bread crumb mixture over the casserole. Bake, uncovered, for 15 minutes or until golden brown and the edges are bubbling.

Baba Ghanouj

Servings: 2

Cooking Time: 40 Minutes

Ingredients:

- 2 Small (12-ounce) purple Italian eggplant(s)
- ¼ cup Olive oil
- ¼ cup Tahini
- ½ teaspoon Ground black pepper
- ¼ teaspoon Onion powder
- ¼ teaspoon Mild smoked paprika (optional)
- Up to 1 teaspoon Table salt

Directions:

1. Preheat the toaster oven to 400°F.
2. Prick the eggplant(s) on all sides with a fork. When the machine is at temperature, set the eggplant(s) in the air fryer oven in one layer. Air-fry undisturbed for 40 minutes, or until blackened and soft.
3. Remove from the machine. Cool the eggplant(s) in the air fryer oven for 20 minutes.
4. Use a nonstick-safe spatula, and perhaps a flatware tablespoon for balance, to gently transfer the eggplant(s) to a bowl. The juices will run out. Make sure the bowl is close to the air fryer oven. Split the eggplant(s) open.
5. Scrape the soft insides of half an eggplant into a food processor. Repeat with the remaining piece(s). Add any juices from the bowl to the eggplant in the food processor, but discard the skins and stems.
6. Add the olive oil, tahini, pepper, onion powder, and smoked paprika (if using). Add about half the salt, then cover and process until

smooth, stopping the machine at least once to scrape down the inside of the canister. Check the spread for salt and add more as needed. Scrape the baba ghanouj into a bowl and serve warm, or set aside at room temperature for up to 2 hours, or cover and store in the refrigerator for up to 4 days.

Asparagus With Pistachio Dukkah

Servings: 3
Cooking Time: 8 Minutes

Ingredients:

- Pistachio Dukkah Ingredients
- 3 tablespoons coriander seeds
- 1 tablespoon cumin seeds
- ½ cup shelled pistachios
- ¼ cup sesame seeds
- 1 teaspoon salt
- ½ teaspoon pepper
- Asparagus Ingredients
- 1 bundle asparagus spears
- 1 tablespoon olive oil
- Salt & pepper, to taste

Directions:

1. Make the pistachio dukkah by placing the coriander and cumin seeds in a skillet over medium heat. Toast for 2 minutes, or until fragrant. Transfer spices to a spice grinder or mortar and pestle. Allow spices to cool completely, then grind.
2. Toast the pistachios in a skillet for 5 minutes, or until golden brown and fragrant. Transfer to a cutting board and chop finely. Add the sesame seeds to the same skillet and toast for 2 minutes, or until golden brown and
3. fragrant. Transfer the pistachios, sesame seeds, coriander, and cumin seeds to a bowl. Add salt and pepper, then stir to combine.
4. Select the Preheat function on the Cosori Smart Air Fryer Toaster Oven, adjust temperature to 430°F, and press Start/Pause.
5. Line the food tray with foil, then place the asparagus on the tray. Drizzle with olive oil and season with salt and pepper.
6. Insert food tray at top position in the preheated oven.
7. Select the Air Fry function, adjust time to 8 minutes, and press Start/Pause.
8. Remove when asparagus is tender. Place asparagus on a serving dish and sprinkle with pistachio dukkah.
9. Pistachio dukkah can be stored at room temperature in a sealed jar or container for up to 4 weeks.

Cauliflower "tater" Tots

Servings: 6
Cooking Time: 10 Minutes

Ingredients:

- 1 head of cauliflower
- 2 eggs
- ¼ cup all-purpose flour
- ½ cup grated Parmesan cheese
- 1 teaspoon salt
- freshly ground black pepper
- vegetable or olive oil, in a spray bottle

Directions:

1. Grate the head of cauliflower with a box grater or finely chop it in a food processor. You should have about 3½ cups. Place the chopped cauliflower in the center of a clean kitchen towel and twist the towel tightly to squeeze all the

water out of the cauliflower. (This can be done in two batches to make it easier to drain all the water from the cauliflower.)

2. Place the squeezed cauliflower in a large bowl. Add the eggs, flour, Parmesan cheese, salt and freshly ground black pepper. Shape the cauliflower into small cylinders or "tater tot" shapes, rolling roughly one tablespoon of the mixture at a time. Place the tots on a cookie sheet lined with paper towel to absorb any residual moisture. Spray the cauliflower tots all over with oil.

3. Preheat the toaster oven to 400°F.

4. Air-fry the tots at 400°F, one layer at a time for 10 minutes, turning them over for the last few minutes of the cooking process for even browning. Season with salt and black pepper. Serve hot with your favorite dipping sauce.

Middle Eastern Phyllo Rolls

Servings: 6

Cooking Time: 5 Minutes

Ingredients:

- 6 ounces Lean ground beef or ground lamb
- 3 tablespoons Sliced almonds
- 1 tablespoon Chutney (any variety), finely chopped
- ¼ teaspoon Ground cinnamon
- ¼ teaspoon Ground coriander
- ¼ teaspoon Ground cumin
- ¼ teaspoon Ground dried turmeric
- ¼ teaspoon Table salt
- ¼ teaspoon Ground black pepper
- 6 18 × 14-inch phyllo sheets (thawed, if necessary)
- Olive oil spray

Directions:

1. Set a medium skillet over medium heat for a minute or two, then crumble in the ground meat. Air-fry for 3 minutes, stirring often, or until well browned. Stir in the almonds, chutney, cinnamon, coriander, cumin, turmeric, salt, and pepper until well combined. Remove from the heat, scrape the cooked ground meat mixture into a bowl, and cool for 15 minutes.

2. Preheat the toaster oven to 400°F.

3. Place one sheet of phyllo dough on a clean, dry work surface. (Keep the others covered.) Lightly coat it with olive oil spray, then fold it in half by bringing the short ends together. Place about 3 tablespoons of the ground meat mixture along one of the longer edges, then fold both of the shorter sides of the dough up and over the meat to partially enclose it (and become a border along the sheet of dough). Roll the dough closed, coat it with olive oil spray on all sides, and set it aside seam side down. Repeat this filling and spraying process with the remaining phyllo sheets.

4. Set the rolls seam side down in the air fryer oven in one layer with some air space between them. Air-fry undisturbed for 5 minutes, or until very crisp and golden brown.

5. Use kitchen tongs to transfer the rolls to a wire rack. Cool for only 2 or 3 minutes before serving hot.

Turkey Burger Sliders

Servings: 8

Cooking Time: 7 Minutes

Ingredients:

- 1 pound ground turkey
- ¼ teaspoon curry powder
- 1 teaspoon Hoisin sauce
- ½ teaspoon salt

- 8 slider buns
- ½ cup slivered red onions
- ½ cup slivered green or red bell pepper
- ½ cup fresh chopped pineapple (or pineapple tidbits from kids' fruit cups, drained)
- light cream cheese, softened

Directions:

1. Combine turkey, curry powder, Hoisin sauce, and salt and mix together well.
2. Shape turkey mixture into 8 small patties.
3. Place patties in air fryer oven and air-fry at 360°F for 7 minutes, until patties are well done and juices run clear.
4. Place each patty on the bottom half of a slider bun and top with onions, peppers, and pineapple. Spread the remaining bun halves with cream cheese to taste, place on top, and serve.

Roasted Brussels Sprouts

Servings: 2

Cooking Time: 30 Minutes

Ingredients:

- 12 ounces brussels sprouts, trimmed and halved
- 4 teaspoons water
- 1 tablespoon extra-virgin olive oil
- ⅛ teaspoon table salt
- Pinch pepper
- Lemon wedges

Directions:

1. Adjust toaster oven rack to middle position and preheat the toaster oven to 450 degrees. Toss brussels sprouts, water, oil, salt, and pepper together on small rimmed baking sheet, then arrange cut side down on sheet in even layer.
2. Cover sheet tightly with aluminum foil and roast for 10 minutes. Remove foil and continue to roast until sprouts are browned and tender, 10 to 15 minutes. Season with salt and pepper. Serve with lemon wedges.

Fried Mozzarella Sticks

Servings: 7

Cooking Time: 5 Minutes

Ingredients:

- 7 1-ounce string cheese sticks, unwrapped
- ½ cup All-purpose flour or tapioca flour
- 2 Large egg(s), well beaten
- 2¼ cups Seasoned Italian-style dried bread crumbs (gluten-free, if a concern)
- Olive oil spray

Directions:

1. Unwrap the string cheese and place the pieces in the freezer for 20 minutes (but not longer, or they will be too frozen to soften in the time given in the air fryer oven).
2. Preheat the toaster oven to 400°F.
3. Set up and fill three shallow soup plates or small pie plates on your counter: one for the flour, one for the egg(s), and one for the bread crumbs.
4. Dip a piece of cold string cheese in the flour until well coated (keep the others in the freezer). Gently tap off any excess flour, then set the stick in the egg(s). Roll it around to coat, let any excess egg mixture slip back into the rest, and set the stick in the bread crumbs. Gently roll it around to coat it evenly, even the ends. Now dip it back in the egg(s), then again in the bread crumbs, rolling it to coat well and evenly. Set the stick aside on a cutting board and coat the remaining pieces of string cheese in the same way.
5. Lightly coat the sticks all over with olive oil spray. Place them in the air fryer oven in one layer

and air-fry undisturbed for 5 minutes, or until golden brown and crisp.

6. Remove from the machine and cool for 5 minutes. Use a nonstick-safe spatula to transfer the mozzarella sticks to a serving platter. Serve hot.

Thick-crust Pepperoni Pizza

Servings: 2

Cooking Time: 10 Minutes

Ingredients:

- 10 ounces Purchased fresh pizza dough (not a prebaked crust)
- Olive oil spray
- ¼ cup Purchased pizza sauce
- 10 slices Sliced pepperoni
- ⅓ cup Purchased shredded Italian 3- or 4-cheese blend

Directions:

1. Preheat the toaster oven to 400°F.
2. Generously coat the inside of a 6-inch round cake pan for a small air fryer oven, a 7-inch round cake pan for a medium air fryer oven, or an 8-inch round cake pan for a large model with olive oil spray.
3. Set the dough in the pan and press it to fill the bottom in an even, thick layer. Spread the sauce over the dough, then top with the pepperoni and cheese.
4. When the machine is at temperature, set the pan in the air fryer oven and air-fry undisturbed for 10 minutes, or until puffed, brown, and bubbling.
5. Use kitchen tongs to transfer the cake pan to a wire rack. Cool for only a minute or so. Use a spatula to loosen the pizza from the pan and lift it out and onto the rack. Continue cooling for a few minutes before cutting into wedges to serve.

Avocado Fries

Servings: 8

Cooking Time: 8 Minutes

Ingredients:

- 2 medium avocados, firm but ripe
- 1 large egg
- ½ teaspoon garlic powder
- ¼ teaspoon cayenne pepper
- ¼ teaspoon salt
- ¾ cup almond flour
- ½ cup finely grated Parmesan cheese
- ½ cup gluten-free breadcrumbs

Directions:

1. Preheat the toaster oven to 370°F.
2. Rinse the outside of the avocado with water. Slice the avocado in half, slice it in half again, and then slice it in half once more to get 8 slices. Remove the outer skin. Repeat for the other avocado. Set the avocado slices aside.
3. In a small bowl, whisk the egg, garlic powder, cayenne pepper, and salt in a small bowl. Set aside.
4. In a separate bowl, pour the almond flour.
5. In a third bowl, mix the Parmesan cheese and breadcrumbs.
6. Carefully roll the avocado slices in the almond flour, then dip them in the egg wash, and coat them in the cheese and breadcrumb topping. Repeat until all 16 fries are coated.
7. Liberally spray the air fryer oven with olive oil spray and place the avocado fries into the air fryer oven, leaving a little space around the sides between fries. Depending on the size of your air fryer oven, you may need to cook these in batches.

8. Cook fries for 8 minutes, or until the outer coating turns light brown.

9. Carefully remove, repeat with remaining slices, and then serve warm.

Cauliflower-crust Pizza

Servings: 3

Cooking Time: 14 Minutes

Ingredients:

- 1 pound 2 ounces Riced cauliflower
- 1 plus 1 large egg yolk Large egg(s)
- 3 tablespoons (a little more than ½ ounce) Finely grated Parmesan cheese
- 1½ tablespoons Potato starch
- ¾ teaspoon Dried oregano
- ¾ teaspoon Table salt
- Vegetable oil spray
- 3 tablespoons Purchased pizza sauce
- 6 tablespoons (about 1½ ounces) Shredded semi-firm mozzarella

Directions:

1. Pour the riced cauliflower into a medium microwave-safe bowl. Microwave on high for 4 minutes. Stir well, then cool for 15 minutes.

2. Preheat the toaster oven to 400°F.

3. Pour the riced cauliflower into a clean kitchen towel or a large piece of cheesecloth. Gather the towel or cheesecloth together. Working over the sink, squeeze the moisture out of the cauliflower, getting out as much of the liquid as you can.

4. Pour the squeezed cauliflower back into that same medium bowl and stir in the egg, egg yolk (if using), cheese, potato starch, oregano, and salt to form a loose, uniform "dough."

5. Cut a piece of aluminum foil or parchment paper into a 6-inch circle for a small pizza, a 7-inch circle for a medium one, or an 8-inch circle for a large one. Coat the circle with vegetable oil spray, then place it in the air-fryer oven. Using a small offset spatula or the back of a flatware tablespoon, spread and smooth the cauliflower mixture onto the circle right to the edges. Air-fry undisturbed for 10 minutes.

6. Remove the pan from the air fryer oven. Reduce the machine's temperature to 350°F .

7. Using a large nonstick-safe spatula, flip over the cauliflower circle along with its foil or parchment paper right in the air fryer oven. Peel off and discard the foil or parchment paper. Spread the pizza sauce evenly over the crust and sprinkle with the cheese.

8. Air-fry undisturbed for 4 minutes, or until the cheese has melted and begun to bubble. Remove the pan from the machine and cool for 5 minutes. Use the same spatula to transfer the pizza to a wire rack to cool for 5 minutes more before cutting the pie into wedges to serve.

Loaded Cauliflower Casserole

Servings: 6

Cooking Time: 35 Minutes

Ingredients:

- Nonstick cooking spray
- 1 cup heavy cream
- 4 tablespoons unsalted butter
- 3 cloves garlic, minced
- 1 teaspoon fresh thyme leaves
- ¾ teaspoon kosher salt
- ¼ teaspoon freshly ground black pepper
- 6 cups cauliflower florets (a medium head)
- ½ cup finely chopped sweet or yellow onion
- 2 cups shredded white cheddar cheese
- 1 ½ cups fresh coarse bread crumbs
- 2 tablespoons sesame seeds

- 3 tablespoons unsalted butter, melted

Directions:

1. Preheat the toaster oven to 425 °F. Spray a 9-inch deep-dish pie plate or 9-inch cake pan with nonstick cooking spray.
2. Bring the cream, butter, garlic, thyme, salt, and pepper to a simmer in a small saucepan over medium heat. Remove from the heat.
3. Place half of the cauliflower into the prepared pan. Sprinkle with half of the onion and half of the cheese. Repeat with the remaining cauliflower, onion, and cheese. Pour the cream mixture over all. Cover and bake until the cauliflower is tender and cooked through, about 20 minutes.
4. Remove the foil and bake for an additional 15 minutes, or until the top is bubbly and beginning to turn golden.
5. Combine the bread crumbs, sesame seeds, and melted butter in a small bowl. Sprinkle over the top and bake for an additional 15 minutes or until golden.

Veggie Cheese Bites

Servings: 4

Cooking Time: 8 Minutes

Ingredients:

- 2 cups riced vegetables
- ½ cup shredded zucchini
- ½ teaspoon garlic powder
- ¼ teaspoon black pepper
- ¼ teaspoon salt
- 1 large egg
- ¾ cup shredded cheddar cheese
- ⅓ cup whole-wheat flour

Directions:

1. Preheat the toaster oven to 350°F.
2. In a large bowl, mix together the riced vegetables, zucchini, garlic powder, pepper, and salt. Mix in the egg. Stir in the shredded cheese and whole-wheat flour until a thick, doughlike consistency forms. If you need to, add 1 teaspoon of flour at a time so you can mold the batter into balls.
3. Using a 1-inch scoop, portion the batter out into about 12 balls.
4. Liberally spray the air fryer oven with olive oil spray. Then place the veggie bites inside. Leave enough room between each bite so the air can flow around them.
5. Air-fry for 8 minutes, or until the outside is slightly browned. Depending on the size of your air fryer oven, you may need to cook these in batches.
6. Remove and let cool slightly before serving.

Crispy Wontons

Servings: 8

Cooking Time: 10 Minutes

Ingredients:

- ½ cup refried beans
- 3 tablespoons salsa
- ¼ cup canned artichoke hearts, drained and patted dry
- ¼ cup frozen spinach, defrosted and squeezed dry
- 2 ounces cream cheese
- 1½ teaspoons dried oregano, divided
- ¼ teaspoon garlic powder
- ¼ teaspoon onion powder
- ½ teaspoon salt
- ¼ cup chopped pepperoni
- ¼ cup grated mozzarella cheese
- 1 tablespoon grated Parmesan

- 2 ounces cream cheese
- ½ teaspoon dried oregano
- 32 wontons
- 1 cup water

Directions:

1. Preheat the toaster oven to 370°F.
2. In a medium bowl, mix together the refried beans and salsa.
3. In a second medium bowl, mix together the artichoke hearts, spinach, cream cheese, oregano, garlic powder, onion powder, and salt.
4. In a third medium bowl, mix together the pepperoni, mozzarella cheese, Parmesan cheese, cream cheese, and the remaining ½ teaspoon of oregano.
5. Get a towel lightly damp with water and ring it out. While working with the wontons, leave the unfilled wontons under the damp towel so they don't dry out.
6. Working with 8 wontons at a time, place 2 teaspoons of one of the fillings into the center of the wonton, rotating among the different fillings (one filling per wonton). Working one at a time, use a pastry brush, dip the pastry brush into the water, and brush the edges of the dough with the water. Fold the dough in half to form a triangle and set aside. Continue until 8 wontons are formed. Spray the wontons with cooking spray and cover with a dry towel. Repeat until all 32 wontons have been filled.
7. Place the wontons into the air fryer oven, leaving space between the wontons, and air-fry for 5 minutes. Turn over and check for brownness, and then air-fry for another 5 minutes.

Mustard Green Beans With Walnuts

Servings: 4

Cooking Time: 20 Minutes

Ingredients:

- 1 ½ pounds fresh green beans, trimmed
- Nonstick cooking spray
- Kosher salt and freshly ground black pepper
- 1 ½ tablespoons white wine vinegar
- 2 tablespoons finely chopped shallots
- 1 ½ tablespoons Dijon mustard
- 1 teaspoon honey
- 2 tablespoons extra-virgin olive oil
- ⅓ cup coarsely chopped walnuts, toasted

Directions:

1. Preheat the toaster oven to 425°F. Place the green beans in a large bowl and spray with nonstick cooking spray. Season with salt and pepper. Place the green beans in a 12 x 12-inch baking pan.
2. Roast for 10 minutes. Stir and roast for an additional 10 minutes, or until the green beans are the desired tenderness.
3. Meanwhile, whisk the vinegar and shallots in a large bowl. Let stand while the green beans are roasting. Whisk the mustard into the vinegar mixture. Stir in the honey. Gradually add the olive oil, whisking until the mixture is thick. Add the green beans; toss gently to coat. Season to taste with additional salt and pepper, if needed. Sprinkle with the walnuts. Serve at room temperature.

Hot Bacon-cheese Dip

Servings: 3

Cooking Time: 30 Minutes

Ingredients:

- Nonstick cooking spray
- 1 (8-ounce) package cream cheese, cut into cubes and softened
- 1 cup sour cream
- 2 tablespoons whole milk
- 1 tablespoon Worcestershire sauce
- ¼ teaspoon Sriracha or hot sauce
- 10 strips bacon, cooked until crisp and crumbled
- 8 ounces shredded sharp cheddar cheese
- 1 green onion, white and green portions, thinly sliced
- Tortilla chips, crackers, broccoli or cauliflower florets, or other favorites, for dipping

Directions:

1. Preheat the toaster oven to 350°F. Spray a 1-quart casserole dish with nonstick cooking spray.
2. Stir the cream cheese, sour cream, milk, Worcestershire sauce, and Sriracha in a medium bowl. Blend well.
3. Reserve 2 tablespoon crumbled bacon for the garnish. Stir the remaining bacon and the cheddar cheese into the cream cheese mixture. Spoon into the prepared dish and cover.
4. Bake for 20 minutes. Stir the dip, cover, and bake for an additional 10 minutes or until hot and melted. Garnish with the reserved bacon and green onion.
5. Serve warm with any of your favorites for dipping.

Creamy Scalloped Potatoes

Servings: 4

Cooking Time: 58 Minutes

Ingredients:

- Oil spray (hand-pumped)
- 2 tablespoons salted butter
- 1 small onion, finely chopped
- 1 teaspoon minced garlic
- 2 tablespoons all-purpose flour
- 1 cup whole milk
- ½ cup low-sodium chicken broth
- ¼ teaspoon ground nutmeg
- ⅛ teaspoon sea salt
- ⅛ teaspoon freshly ground black pepper
- 1½ pounds russet potatoes, cut into ⅛-inch-thick slices

Directions:

1. Place the rack on position 1 and preheat the toaster oven on BAKE to 350°F for 5 minutes.
2. Lightly spray an 8-inch-square baking dish with oil and set aside.
3. Melt the butter in a medium saucepan over medium-high heat. Sauté the onion and garlic in the butter until softened, about 4 minutes. Add the flour and cook, whisking, for 1 minute.
4. Whisk in the milk and chicken broth until well blended and cook, whisking constantly, until thickened, about 3 minutes. Remove the sauce from the heat and whisk in the nutmeg, salt, and pepper. Set aside.
5. Layer one-third of the potato slices in the baking dish and top with one-third of the sauce. Repeat the layering in thirds, ending with the cream sauce.
6. Cover the dish with aluminum foil and bake for 25 minutes. Remove the foil and bake for an additional 25 minutes until golden brown and the potatoes are tender. Serve.

Corn Dog Muffins

Servings: 8

Cooking Time: 10 Minutes

Ingredients:

- 1¼ cups sliced kosher hotdogs (3 or 4, depending on size)
- ½ cup flour
- ½ cup yellow cornmeal
- 2 teaspoons baking powder
- ½ cup skim milk
- 1 egg
- 2 tablespoons canola oil
- 8 foil muffin cups, paper liners removed
- cooking spray
- mustard or your favorite dipping sauce

Directions:

1. Slice each hot dog in half lengthwise, then cut in ¼-inch half-moon slices. Set aside.
2. Preheat the toaster oven to 390°F.
3. In a large bowl, stir together flour, cornmeal, and baking powder.
4. In a small bowl, beat together the milk, egg, and oil until just blended.
5. Pour egg mixture into dry ingredients and stir with a spoon to mix well.
6. Stir in sliced hot dogs.
7. Spray the foil cups lightly with cooking spray.
8. Divide mixture evenly into muffin cups.
9. Place 4 muffin cups in the air fryer oven and air-fry for 5 minutes.
10. Reduce temperature to 360°F and cook 5 minutes or until toothpick inserted in center of muffin comes out clean.
11. Repeat steps 9 and 10 to bake remaining corn dog muffins.
12. Serve with mustard or other sauces for dipping.

Easy Baked Potato

Servings: 4

Cooking Time: 60minutes

Ingredients:

- 2 tablespoons table salt for brining
- 1 (7- to 9-ounce) russet potato, unpeeled, lightly pricked with fork in 6 places
- 1 teaspoon vegetable oil

Directions:

1. Adjust toaster oven rack to middle position and preheat the toaster oven to 450 degrees. Dissolve salt in ½ cup water in large bowl. Place potato in bowl and toss so exterior of potato is evenly moistened. Transfer potato to small wire rack set in small rimmed baking sheet and bake until center of potato registers 205 degrees, 45 minutes to 1 hour.
2. Remove potato from oven and brush tops and sides with oil. Return potato to oven and continue to bake for 10 minutes.
3. Remove potato from oven and, using paring knife, make 2 slits, forming X, in potato. Using clean dish towel, hold ends and squeeze slightly to push flesh up and out. Season with salt and pepper to taste. Serve immediately.

Spicy Pigs In A Blanket

Servings: 20

Cooking Time: 15 Minutes

Ingredients:

- 6 tablespoons unsalted butter, melted
- 1 teaspoon poppy seeds
- 1 teaspoon dry minced onion
- ½ teaspoon granulated garlic
- ½ teaspoon dry mustard
- ¼ teaspoon red pepper flakes

- 1 (8-ounce) tube refrigerated crescent dough sheets
- 1 (12-ounce) package cocktail smoked sausages

Directions:

1. Combine the butter, poppy seeds, onion, garlic, dry mustard, and red pepper flakes in a small bowl.
2. Lightly flour a clean surface and unroll the crescent roll sheet. Cut the sheet in half down the center, then cut those pieces in half the other way. Continue to make vertical and horizontal cuts until you have 32 strips of dough.
3. Preheat the toaster oven to 375°F.
4. Drain and pat dry the cocktail sausages using paper towels. Wrap each sausage in a strip of dough. Place about half on a 12 x 12-inch baking pan, seam side down.
5. Stir the butter mixture again to distribute all the spices and brush generously over the pastry-wrapped sausages. Bake for 14 to 15 minutes, or until they are golden brown. Repeat with the remaining half of the ingredients. Allow to cool slightly before serving.

Cinnamon Apple Chips

Servings: 4

Cooking Time: 480 Minutes

Ingredients:

- 1 apple
- 1 tablespoon lemon juice
- ¼ teaspoon cinnamon

Directions:

1. Slice the apple into ⅛-inch-thick slices, preferably by using a mandoline slicer.
2. Place slices in a bowl of water mixed with the lemon juice to prevent browning. Remove after 2 minutes and dry thoroughly with paper towels.
3. Sprinkle the apple slices with cinnamon and place on the food tray.
4. Insert the food tray at mid position in the preheated oven.
5. Preheat the toaster oven to 130°F.
6. Remove when apple chips are crispy.

Rosemary-roasted Potatoes

Servings:4

Cooking Time: 40 Minutes

Ingredients:

- 1 pound russet potatoes, or baby potatoes, cut into 1-inch chunks
- 2 tablespoons olive oil
- 1 teaspoon garlic powder
- 1 teaspoon dried rosemary
- Sea salt, for seasoning
- Freshly ground black pepper, for seasoning

Directions:

1. Preheat the toaster oven on AIR FRY to 400°F for 5 minutes.
2. In a large bowl, toss the potatoes with the oil, garlic powder, and rosemary. Season with salt and pepper.
3. Place the air-fryer basket in the baking tray and spread the potatoes in a single layer in the basket. You may have to do two batches. Cover the first batch loosely with foil to keep it warm while you cook the second batch.
4. In position 2, AIR FRY on 400°F for 20 minutes, shaking the basket at 10 minutes, until the potatoes are tender and golden brown. Repeat with the remaining potatoes and serve.

Sweet Chili– Glazed Wings

Servings: 4

Cooking Time: 27 Minutes

Ingredients:

- 1 pound chicken wing drumettes
- ½ cup reduced-sodium soy sauce
- 3 tablespoons honey
- 3 tablespoons unseasoned rice vinegar
- 1 tablespoon sesame oil
- 1 ½ teaspoons chili garlic paste
- ¼ teaspoon freshly ground black pepper
- ¼ cup jarred Asian sweet chili sauce

Directions:

1. Place the chicken drumettes in a deep bowl. Stir the soy sauce, honey, rice vinegar, sesame oil, chili garlic paste, and pepper in a small bowl. Pour the soy sauce mixture over the chicken. Cover the bowl and refrigerate for several hours or overnight.
2. Preheat the toaster oven to 375°F. Line a 12 x 12-inch baking pan with aluminum foil.
3. Drain and discard the marinade. Pat the chicken dry and arrange in a single layer in the prepared pan. Bake, uncovered, for 18 to 20 minutes or until lightly browned and almost done.
4. Brush the chicken with the sweet chili sauce, turning to coat evenly. Bake for 6 to 7 minutes or until the chicken is done, a meat thermometer registers 165°F, and the edges are beginning to crisp.

Foolproof Baked White Rice

Servings: 2

Cooking Time: 45 Minutes

Ingredients:

- 1¾ cups boiling water
- 1 cup long-grain white rice, rinsed
- 1 teaspoon extra-virgin olive oil
- ¼ teaspoon table salt

Directions:

1. Adjust toaster oven rack to middle position and preheat the toaster oven to 450 degrees. Combine all ingredients in 8-inch square baking dish or pan. Cover dish tightly with aluminum foil and bake until liquid is absorbed and rice is tender, 20 to 30 minutes, rotating dish halfway through baking.
2. Remove dish from oven, uncover, and fluff rice with fork, scraping up any rice that has stuck to bottom. Re-cover dish with foil and let rice sit for 10 minutes. Season with salt and pepper to taste. Serve.

FISH AND SEAFOOD

Lobster Tails

Servings: 4

Cooking Time: 10 Minutes

Ingredients:

- Brushing mixture:
- 2 tablespoons lemon juice
- 2 tablespoons olive oil
- ½ teaspoon garlic powder
- ¼ teaspoon ground thyme
- 4 6-ounce lobster tails

Directions:

1. Whisk together the brushing mixture ingredients in a small bowl and set aside. CUT the top of each lobster shell lengthwise from the top edge to the tail with a sharp scissors. Place the lobster tails, cut side down, on a broiling rack with a pan underneath. Brush with the brushing mixture.
2. BROIL for 5 minutes. Remove from the oven and brush again. Broil for 5 minutes, or until the lobster flesh turns from translucent to opaque.

Butternut Squash–wrapped Halibut Fillets

Servings: 3

Cooking Time: 11 Minutes

Ingredients:

- 15 Long spiralized peeled and seeded butternut squash strands
- 3 5- to 6-ounce skinless halibut fillets
- 3 tablespoons Butter, melted
- ¾ teaspoon Mild paprika
- ¾ teaspoon Table salt
- ¾ teaspoon Ground black pepper

Directions:

1. Preheat the toaster oven to 375°F .
2. Hold 5 long butternut squash strands together and wrap them around a fillet. Set it aside and wrap any remaining fillet(s).
3. Mix the melted butter, paprika, salt, and pepper in a small bowl. Brush this mixture over the squash-wrapped fillets on all sides.
4. When the machine is at temperature, set the fillets in the air fryer oven with as much air space between them as possible. Air-fry undisturbed for 10 minutes, or until the squash strands have browned but not burned. If the machine is at 360°F, you may need to add 1 minute to the cooking time. In any event, watch the fish carefully after the 8-minute mark.
5. Use a nonstick-safe spatula to gently transfer the fillets to a serving platter or plates. Cool for only a minute or so before serving.

Beer-breaded Halibut Fish Tacos

Servings: 4

Cooking Time: 10 Minutes

Ingredients:

- 1 pound halibut, cut into 1-inch strips
- 1 cup light beer
- 1 jalapeño, minced and divided
- 1 clove garlic, minced
- ¼ teaspoon ground cumin
- ½ cup cornmeal
- ¼ cup all-purpose flour
- 1¼ teaspoons sea salt, divided
- 2 cups shredded cabbage
- 1 lime, juiced and divided

- ¼ cup Greek yogurt
- ¼ cup mayonnaise
- 1 cup grape tomatoes, quartered
- ½ cup chopped cilantro
- ¼ cup chopped onion
- 1 egg, whisked
- 8 corn tortillas

Directions:

1. In a shallow baking dish, place the fish, the beer, 1 teaspoon of the minced jalapeño, the garlic, and the cumin. Cover and refrigerate for 30 minutes.
2. Meanwhile, in a medium bowl, mix together the cornmeal, flour, and ½ teaspoon of the salt.
3. In large bowl, mix together the shredded cabbage, 1 tablespoon of the lime juice, the Greek yogurt, the mayonnaise, and ½ teaspoon of the salt.
4. In a small bowl, make the pico de gallo by mixing together the tomatoes, cilantro, onion, ¼ teaspoon of the salt, the remaining jalapeño, and the remaining lime juice.
5. Remove the fish from the refrigerator and discard the marinade. Dredge the fish in the whisked egg; then dredge the fish in the cornmeal flour mixture, until all pieces of fish have been breaded.
6. Preheat the toaster oven to 350°F.
7. Place the fish in the air fryer oven and spray liberally with cooking spray. Air-fry for 6 minutes, flip the fish, and cook another 4 minutes.
8. While the fish is cooking, heat the tortillas in a heavy skillet for 1 to 2 minutes over high heat.
9. To assemble the tacos, place the battered fish on the heated tortillas, and top with slaw and pico de gallo. Serve immediately.

Roasted Fish With Provençal Crumb Topping

Servings: 3

Cooking Time: 25 Minutes

Ingredients:

- 1 tablespoon olive oil, plus more for greasing
- ⅓ cup finely chopped onion
- 1 clove garlic, minced
- ¾ cup fresh bread crumbs
- 2 tablespoons chopped fresh flat-leaf (Italian) parsley
- 1 teaspoon fresh thyme leaves
- 3 (5-ounce) cod fillets, or other white-fleshed, mild-flavored fish, patted dry (about 1 ¼ inches thick)
- 2 tablespoons dry white wine
- 2 teaspoons fresh lemon juice

Directions:

1. Preheat the toaster oven to 400°F. Lightly grease the baking pan with olive oil.
2. Heat the tablespoon of olive oil in a small skillet over medium-high heat. Add the onion and cook, stirring frequently, for 3 to 4 minutes, or until tender. Add the garlic and cook for 30 seconds. Remove the skillet from the heat. Stir in the bread crumbs, parsley, and thyme.
3. Place the fish in the prepared pan. Drizzle with the wine. Divide the crumb mixture evenly over the top of each fish fillet, and press onto the fillets. Roast for 20 to 25 minutes, or until the top is brown and the fish is opaque and flakes easily when tested with a fork. Sprinkle the lemon juice evenly over the fish.

Tuna Nuggets In Hoisin Sauce

Servings: 4

Cooking Time: 7 Minutes

Ingredients:

- ½ cup hoisin sauce
- 2 tablespoons rice wine vinegar
- 2 teaspoons sesame oil
- 1 teaspoon garlic powder
- 2 teaspoons dried lemongrass
- ¼ teaspoon red pepper flakes
- ½ small onion, quartered and thinly sliced
- 8 ounces fresh tuna, cut into 1-inch cubes
- cooking spray
- 3 cups cooked jasmine rice

Directions:

1. Mix the hoisin sauce, vinegar, sesame oil, and seasonings together.
2. Stir in the onions and tuna nuggets.
3. Spray air fryer oven baking pan with nonstick spray and pour in tuna mixture.
4. Air-fry at 390°F for 3 minutes. Stir gently.
5. Cook 2 minutes and stir again, checking for doneness. Tuna should be barely cooked through, just beginning to flake and still very moist. If necessary, continue cooking and stirring in 1-minute intervals until done.
6. Serve warm over hot jasmine rice.

Fish And "chips"

Servings: 2

Cooking Time: 10 Minutes

Ingredients:

- ½ cup flour
- ½ teaspoon paprika
- ¼ teaspoon ground white pepper (or freshly ground black pepper)
- 1 egg
- ¼ cup mayonnaise
- 2 cups salt & vinegar kettle cooked potato chips, coarsely crushed
- 12 ounces cod
- tartar sauce
- lemon wedges

Directions:

1. Set up a dredging station. Combine the flour, paprika and pepper in a shallow dish. Combine the egg and mayonnaise in a second shallow dish. Place the crushed potato chips in a third shallow dish.
2. Cut the cod into 6 pieces. Dredge each piece of fish in the flour, then dip it into the egg mixture and then place it into the crushed potato chips. Make sure all sides of the fish are covered and pat the chips gently onto the fish so they stick well.
3. Preheat the toaster oven to 370°F.
4. Place the coated fish fillets into the air fry oven. (It is ok if a couple of pieces slightly overlap or rest on top of other fillets in order to fit everything in the air fryer oven.)
5. Air-fry for 10 minutes, gently turning the fish over halfway through the cooking time.
6. Transfer the fish to a platter and serve with tartar sauce and lemon wedges.

Crispy Sweet-and-sour Cod Fillets

Servings: 3

Cooking Time: 12 Minutes

Ingredients:

- 1½ cups Plain panko bread crumbs (gluten-free, if a concern)

- 2 tablespoons Regular or low-fat mayonnaise (not fat-free; gluten-free, if a concern)
- ¼ cup Sweet pickle relish
- 3 4- to 5-ounce skinless cod fillets

Directions:

1. Preheat the toaster oven to 400°F.
2. Pour the bread crumbs into a shallow soup plate or a small pie plate. Mix the mayonnaise and relish in a small bowl until well combined. Smear this mixture all over the cod fillets. Set them in the crumbs and turn until evenly coated on all sides, even on the ends.
3. Set the coated cod fillets in the air fryer oven with as much air space between them as possible. They should not touch. Air-fry undisturbed for 12 minutes, or until browned and crisp.
4. Use a nonstick-safe spatula to transfer the cod pieces to a wire rack. Cool for only a minute or two before serving hot.

Coconut-crusted Shrimp

Servings: 4

Cooking Time: 20 Minutes

Ingredients:

- Oil spray (hand-pumped)
- ½ cup all-purpose flour
- 2 large eggs
- ¾ cup unsweetened, shredded coconut
- ½ cup panko bread crumbs
- ¼ teaspoon sea salt
- 1 pound (26 to 30 count) raw extra-large shrimp, peeled and deveined with tails attached

Directions:

1. Preheat the toaster oven to 400°F on AIR FRY for 5 minutes.
2. Place the air-fryer basket in the baking tray and spray it generously with the oil.
3. Place the flour on a plate and set it on your work surface.
4. In a small bowl, whisk the eggs until well beaten and place next to the flour.
5. In a medium bowl, stir the coconut, bread crumbs, and salt, and place next to the eggs.
6. Pat the shrimp dry with paper towels. Working in two batches, dredge the shrimp in the flour, then egg, then coconut mixture, and place them in the basket. Do not crowd the basket.
7. Lightly spray the shrimp with the oil on both sides and in position 2, air fry for 10 minutes, turning halfway through, until golden brown.
8. Repeat with the remaining shrimp, covering the cooked shrimp loosely with foil to keep them warm. Serve.

Sea Scallops

Servings: 4

Cooking Time: 8 Minutes

Ingredients:

- 1½ pounds sea scallops
- salt and pepper
- 2 eggs
- ½ cup flour
- ½ cup plain breadcrumbs
- oil for misting or cooking spray

Directions:

1. Rinse scallops and remove the tough side muscle. Sprinkle to taste with salt and pepper.
2. Beat eggs together in a shallow dish. Place flour in a second shallow dish and breadcrumbs in a third.
3. Preheat the toaster oven to 390°F.
4. Dip scallops in flour, then eggs, and then roll in breadcrumbs. Mist with oil or cooking spray.

5. Place scallops in air fryer oven in a single layer, leaving some space between. You should be able to cook about a dozen at a time.

6. Air-fry at 390°F for 8 minutes, watching carefully so as not to overcook. Scallops are done when they turn opaque all the way through. They will feel slightly firm when pressed with tines of a fork.

7. Repeat step 6 to cook remaining scallops.

Broiled Scallops

Servings: 6

Cooking Time: 3 Minutes

Ingredients:

- Broiling sauce:
- 2 tablespoons chopped fresh parsley
- 3 shallots, finely chopped
- ¾ cup white wine
- 3 tablespoons margarine, at room
- Temperature
- ½ teaspoon dried thyme
- 3 tablespoons sesame seeds
- Salt and freshly ground black pepper
- 1½ pounds (3 cups) bay scallops, rinsed and drained

Directions:

1. Whisk together the ingredients for the broiling sauce in a small bowl and transfer to a 1-quart 8½ × 8½ × 4-inch ovenproof baking dish. Adjust the seasoning, add the scallops, and spoon the mixture over them.

2. BROIL for 3 minutes, or until all the scallops are opaque instead of translucent. Serve with the sauce.

Maple-crusted Salmon

Servings: 2

Cooking Time: 8 Minutes

Ingredients:

- 12 ounces salmon filets
- ⅓ cup maple syrup
- 1 teaspoon Worcestershire sauce
- 2 teaspoons Dijon mustard or brown mustard
- ½ cup finely chopped walnuts
- ½ teaspoon sea salt
- ½ lemon
- 1 tablespoon chopped parsley, for garnish

Directions:

1. Place the salmon in a shallow baking dish. Top with maple syrup, Worcestershire sauce, and mustard. Refrigerate for 30 minutes.

2. Preheat the toaster oven to 350°F.

3. Remove the salmon from the marinade and discard the marinade.

4. Place the chopped nuts on top of the salmon filets, and sprinkle salt on top of the nuts. Place the salmon, skin side down, in the air fryer oven. Air-fry for 6 to 8 minutes or until the fish flakes in the center.

5. Remove the salmon and plate on a serving platter. Squeeze fresh lemon over the top of the salmon and top with chopped parsley. Serve immediately.

Oven-crisped Fish Fillets With Salsa

Servings: 4

Cooking Time: 14 Minutes

Ingredients:

- Coating ingredients:
- 1 cup cornmeal
- 1 teaspoon garlic powder
- 1 teaspoon ground cumin

- 1 teaspoon paprika
- Salt to taste
- 4 6-ounce fish fillets, approximately
- ¼ to ½ inch thick
- 2 tablespoons vegetable oil

Directions:

1. Combine the coating ingredients in a small bowl, blending well. Transfer to a large plate, spreading evenly over the surface. Brush the fillets with vegetable oil and press both sides of each fillet into the coating.
2. BROIL an oiled or nonstick 8½ × 8½ × 2-inch square baking (cake) pan for 1 or 2 minutes to preheat. Remove the pan and place the fillets in the hot pan, laying them flat.
3. BROIL for 7 minutes, then remove the pan from the oven and carefully turn the fillets with a spatula. Broil for another 7 minutes, or until the fish flakes easily with a fork and the coating is crisped to your preference. Serve immediately.

Quick Shrimp Scampi

Servings: 2

Cooking Time: 5 Minutes

Ingredients:

- 16 to 20 raw large shrimp, peeled, deveined and tails removed
- ½ cup white wine
- freshly ground black pepper
- ¼ cup + 1 tablespoon butter, divided
- 1 clove garlic, sliced
- 1 teaspoon olive oil
- salt, to taste
- juice of ½ lemon, to taste
- ¼ cup chopped fresh parsley

Directions:

1. Start by marinating the shrimp in the white wine and freshly ground black pepper for at least 30 minutes, or as long as 2 hours in the refrigerator.
2. Preheat the toaster oven to 400°F.
3. Melt ¼ cup of butter in a small saucepan on the stovetop. Add the garlic and let the butter simmer, but be sure to not let it burn.
4. Pour the shrimp and marinade into the air fryer oven, letting the marinade drain through to the bottom drawer. Drizzle the olive oil on the shrimp and season well with salt. Air-fry at 400°F for 3 minutes. Turn the shrimp over and pour the garlic butter over the shrimp. Air-fry for another 2 minutes.
5. Remove the shrimp from the air fryer oven and transfer them to a bowl. Squeeze lemon juice over all the shrimp and toss with the chopped parsley and remaining tablespoon of butter. Season to taste with salt and serve immediately.

Roasted Garlic Shrimp

Servings: 4

Cooking Time: 12 Minutes

Ingredients:

- Nonstick cooking spray
- ¼ cup unsalted butter, melted
- 2 cloves garlic, minced
- 1 teaspoon grated lemon zest
- ½ teaspoon dried thyme leaves
- ¼ teaspoon freshly ground black pepper
- Kosher salt
- 1 pound uncooked large shrimp, fresh or frozen and thawed, peeled and deveined
- 1 ½ tablespoons fresh lemon juice
- Optional: Minced fresh flat-leaf (Italian) parsley

Directions:

1. Preheat the toaster oven to 400°F. Spray a 12 x 12-inch baking pan with nonstick cooking spray.
2. Mix the melted butter, garlic, lemon zest, thyme, and pepper in a small bowl. Season with salt. Set aside.
3. Arrange the shrimp in a single layer in the prepared pan. Pour the butter mixture over the shrimp, then stir gently to coat the shrimp.
4. Roast, uncovered, for 10 to 12 minutes or until the shrimp turn pink. Drizzle with the lemon juice. Transfer to a serving platter and spoon any collected drippings over the shrimp. Garnish, if desired, with minced parsley.

Baked Parsley Mussels With Zucchini

Servings: 6

Cooking Time: 40 Minutes

Ingredients:

- 2 pounds (approximately 40) mussels, cooked, shells discarded
- 4 small zucchini squash, scrubbed, halved, and cut lengthwise into ½-inch-wide strips
- ½ cup dry white wine
- 1 tablespoon chopped fresh oregano or 1 teaspoon dried oregano
- 2 garlic cloves, minced
- ¼ cup chopped fresh Italian parsley
- 2 tablespoons olive oil
- Freshly ground black pepper to taste
- ¼ cup grated low-fat Parmesan cheese

Directions:

1. Preheat the toaster oven to 350° F.
2. Combine all the ingredients except the Parmesan cheese in a 1-quart 8½ × 8½ × 4-inch ovenproof baking dish, mixing well. Adjust the seasonings to taste and cover with aluminum foil.
3. BAKE for 35 minutes, or until the zucchini is tender. Uncover and sprinkle with Parmesan cheese.
4. BROIL for 5 minutes, or until the cheese is melted and the top is lightly browned.

Crispy Smelts

Servings: 3

Cooking Time: 20 Minutes

Ingredients:

- 1 pound Cleaned smelts
- 3 tablespoons Tapioca flour
- Vegetable oil spray
- To taste Coarse sea salt or kosher salt

Directions:

1. Preheat the toaster oven to 400°F.
2. Toss the smelts and tapioca flour in a large bowl until the little fish are evenly coated.
3. Lay the smelts out on a large cutting board. Lightly coat both sides of each fish with vegetable oil spray.
4. When the machine is at temperature, set the smelts close together in the air fryer oven, with a few even overlapping on top. Air-fry undisturbed for 20 minutes, until lightly browned and crisp.
5. Remove from the machine and turn out the fish onto a wire rack. The smelts will most likely come out as one large block, or maybe in a couple of large pieces. Cool for a minute or two, then sprinkle the smelts with salt and break the block(s) into much smaller sections or individual fish to serve.

Oysters Broiled In Wine Sauce

Servings: 2

Cooking Time: 20 Minutes

Ingredients:

- Sauce:
- 2 tablespoons margarine, at room temperature
- 1 cup dry white wine
- 3 garlic cloves, minced
- Salt and freshly ground black pepper to taste
- 24 fresh oysters, shucked and drained

Directions:

1. Combine the sauce ingredients in a 1-quart 8½ × 8½ × 4-inch ovenproof baking dish and adjust the seasonings to taste.
2. BROIL the sauce for 5 minutes, remove the pan from the oven, and stir. Return to the oven and broil for another 5 minutes, or until the sauce begins to bubble. Remove from the oven and cool for 5 minutes. Add the oysters, spooning the sauce over them to cover thoroughly.
3. BROIL for 5 minutes, or until the oysters are just cooked.

Almond-crusted Fish

Servings: 4

Cooking Time: 10 Minutes

Ingredients:

- 4 4-ounce fish fillets
- ¾ cup breadcrumbs
- ¼ cup sliced almonds, crushed
- 2 tablespoons lemon juice
- ⅛ teaspoon cayenne
- salt and pepper
- ¾ cup flour
- 1 egg, beaten with 1 tablespoon water
- oil for misting or cooking spray

Directions:

1. Split fish fillets lengthwise down the center to create 8 pieces.
2. Mix breadcrumbs and almonds together and set aside.
3. Mix the lemon juice and cayenne together. Brush on all sides of fish.
4. Season fish to taste with salt and pepper.
5. Place the flour on a sheet of wax paper.
6. Roll fillets in flour, dip in egg wash, and roll in the crumb mixture.
7. Mist both sides of fish with oil or cooking spray.
8. Spray air fryer oven and lay fillets inside.
9. Air-fry at 390°F for 5 minutes, turn fish over, and air-fry for an additional 5 minutes or until fish is done and flakes easily.

Sweet Chili Shrimp

Servings: 4

Cooking Time: 6 Minutes

Ingredients:

- 1 pound jumbo shrimp, peeled and deveined
- ¼ cup sweet chili sauce
- 1 lime, zested and juiced
- 1 tablespoon soy sauce
- 1 tablespoon honey
- 1 tablespoon olive oil
- 1 large garlic clove, minced
- ½ teaspoon salt
- ¼ teaspoon pepper
- 1 green onion, thinly sliced, for garnish

Directions:

1. Place the shrimp in a large bowl. Whisk all the remaining ingredients except the green onion in a separate bowl.
2. Pour sauce over the shrimp and toss to coat.

3. Preheat the toaster Oven to 430°F.
4. Line the food tray with foil, place shrimp on the tray, then insert at top position in the preheated oven.
5. Select the Air Fry function, adjust time to 6 minutes, and press Start/Pause.
6. Remove shrimp and garnish with sliced green onions.

Crab-stuffed Peppers

Servings: 4

Cooking Time: 45 Minutes

Ingredients:

- Filling:
- 1½ cups fresh crabmeat, chopped, or 2 6-ounce cans lump crabmeat, drained
- 4 plum tomatoes, chopped
- 2 4-ounce cans sliced mushrooms, drained well
- 4 tablespoons pitted and sliced black olives
- 2 tablespoons olive oil
- 2 garlic cloves, minced
- ½ teaspoon ground cumin
- Salt and freshly ground black pepper to taste
- 4 large bell peppers, tops cut off, seeds and membrane removed
- ½ cup shredded low-fat mozzarella cheese

Directions:

1. Preheat the toaster oven to 375° F.
2. Combine the filling ingredients in a bowl and adjust the seasonings. Spoon the mixture to generously fill each pepper. Place the peppers upright in an 8½ × 8½ × 2-inch oiled or nonstick square (cake) pan.
3. BAKE for 40 minutes, or until the peppers are tender. Remove from the oven and sprinkle the cheese in equal portions on top of the peppers.
4. BROIL 5 minutes, or until the cheese is melted.

Skewered Salsa Verde Shrimp

Servings: 4

Cooking Time: 8 Minutes

Ingredients:

- 1½ pounds large fresh shrimp, peeled and deveined
- Brushing mixture:
- 1 7-ounce can salsa verde
- 1 teaspoon ground cumin
- ½ teaspoon chopped fresh cilantro or parsley
- 1 teaspoon garlic powder
- 3 tablespoons plain yogurt
- 1 tablespoon olive oil
- Lemon wedges

Directions:

1. Thread the shrimp onto the skewers.
2. Combine the brushing mixture ingredients in a small bowl. Adjust the seasonings and brush the shrimp with the mixture.
3. BROIL the shrimp for 4 minutes. Turn the skewers, brush the shrimp again, and broil for another 4 minutes, or until the shrimp are firm and cooked. Remove the shrimp from the skewers and serve with lemon wedges.

Pecan-crusted Tilapia

Servings: 4

Cooking Time: 8 Minutes

Ingredients:

- 1 pound skinless, boneless tilapia filets
- ¼ cup butter, melted
- 1 teaspoon minced fresh or dried rosemary
- 1 cup finely chopped pecans
- 1 teaspoon sea salt

- ¼ teaspoon paprika
- 2 tablespoons chopped parsley
- 1 lemon, cut into wedges

Directions:

1. Pat the tilapia filets dry with paper towels.
2. Pour the melted butter over the filets and flip the filets to coat them completely.
3. In a medium bowl, mix together the rosemary, pecans, salt, and paprika.
4. Preheat the toaster oven to 350°F.
5. Place the tilapia filets into the air fryer oven and top with the pecan coating. Air-fry for 6 to 8 minutes. The fish should be firm to the touch and flake easily when fully cooked.
6. Remove the fish from the air fryer oven. Top the fish with chopped parsley and serve with lemon wedges.

Blackened Red Snapper

Servings: 4

Cooking Time: 8 Minutes

Ingredients:

- 1½ teaspoons black pepper
- ¼ teaspoon thyme
- ¼ teaspoon garlic powder
- ⅛ teaspoon cayenne pepper
- 1 teaspoon olive oil
- 4 4-ounce red snapper fillet portions, skin on
- 4 thin slices lemon
- cooking spray

Directions:

1. Mix the spices and oil together to make a paste. Rub into both sides of the fish.
2. Spray air fryer oven with nonstick cooking spray and lay snapper steaks in air fryer oven, skin-side down.
3. Place a lemon slice on each piece of fish.
4. Air-fry at 390°F for 8 minutes. The fish will not flake when done, but it should be white through the center.

Lightened-up Breaded Fish Filets

Servings: 4

Cooking Time: 10 Minutes

Ingredients:

- ½ cup all-purpose flour
- ½ teaspoon cayenne pepper
- 1 teaspoon garlic powder
- ½ teaspoon black pepper
- ¼ teaspoon salt
- 2 eggs, whisked
- 1½ cups panko breadcrumbs
- 1 pound boneless white fish filets
- 1 cup tartar sauce
- 1 lemon, sliced into wedges

Directions:

1. In a medium bowl, mix the flour, cayenne pepper, garlic powder, pepper, and salt.
2. In a shallow dish, place the eggs.
3. In a third dish, place the breadcrumbs.
4. Cover the fish in the flour, dip them in the egg, and coat them with panko. Repeat until all fish are covered in the breading.
5. Liberally spray the metal trivet that fits inside the air fryer oven with olive oil mist. Place the fish onto the trivet, leaving space between the filets to flip. Air-fry for 5 minutes, flip the fish, and cook another 5 minutes. Repeat until all the fish is cooked.
6. Serve warm with tartar sauce and lemon wedges.

Fish With Sun-dried Tomato Pesto

Servings: 4

Cooking Time: 31 Minutes

Ingredients:

- Tomato sauce:
- ¼ cup chopped sun-dried tomatoes
- 2 tablespoons chopped fresh basil
- ⅔ cup dry white wine
- 2 tablespoons grated Parmesan cheese
- 2 tablespoons olive oil
- 1 tablespoon pine nuts
- 2 garlic cloves
- Salt and freshly ground black pepper to taste
- 4 6-ounce fish fillets (trout, catfish, flounder, or tilapia)
- 1 tablespoon reduced-fat mayonnaise
- 2 tablespoons chopped fresh cilantro Olive oil

Directions:

1. Preheat the toaster oven to 400° F.
2. Process the tomato sauce ingredients in a blender or food processor until smooth.
3. Layer the fish fillets in an oiled or nonstick 8½ × 8½ × 2-inch square baking (cake) pan. Spoon the sauce over the fish, spreading evenly.
4. BAKE, uncovered, for 25 minutes, or until the fish flakes easily with a fork. Remove from the oven, spread the mayonnaise on top of the fish, and garnish with the cilantro.
5. BROIL for 6 minutes, or until lightly browned.

Oven-poached Salmon

Servings: 2

Cooking Time: 20 Minutes

Ingredients:

- Poaching liquid:
- 1 cup dry white wine
- 2 bay leaves
- 1 tablespoon mustard seed
- Salt and freshly ground black pepper to taste
- 2 6-ounce salmon steaks
- 2 tablespoons fresh watercress, rinsed, drained, and chopped (for serving hot)
- 1 lemon, cut into small wedges (for serving hot)
- Cucumber Sauce (recipe follows)

Directions:

1. Preheat the toaster oven to 350° F.
2. Combine the poaching liquid ingredients with 1 cup water in a small bowl and set aside.
3. Place the salmon steaks in an oiled or nonstick 8½ × 8½ × 2-inch square baking (cake) pan and pour enough poaching liquid over the steaks to barely cover them. Adjust the seasonings to taste.
4. BAKE, uncovered, for 20 minutes, or until the fish feels springy to the touch. Remove the bay leaves and serve the fish hot with watercress and lemon or cold with Cucumber Sauce.

Crab Cakes

Servings: 4

Cooking Time: 9 Minutes

Ingredients:

- 1 pound lump crab meat, checked for shells
- ⅓ cup breadcrumbs
- ¼ cup finely chopped onions
- ¼ cup finely chopped red bell peppers
- ¼ cup finely chopped parsley
- ¼ teaspoon sea salt
- 2 eggs, whisked
- ¾ cup mayonnaise, divided

- ¼ cup sour cream
- 1 lemon, divided
- ¼ cup sweet pickle relish
- 1 tablespoon prepared mustard

Directions:

1. In a large bowl, mix together the crab meat, breadcrumbs, onions, bell peppers, parsley, sea salt, eggs, and ¼ cup of the mayonnaise.
2. Preheat the toaster oven to 380°F.
3. Form 8 patties with the crab cake mixture. Line the air fryer oven with parchment paper and place the crab cakes on the parchment paper. Spray with cooking spray. Air-fry for 4 minutes, turn over the crab cakes, spray with cooking spray, and air-fry for an additional 3 to 5 minutes, or until golden brown and the edges are crispy. Cook in batches as needed.
4. Meanwhile, make the sauce. In a small bowl, mix together the remaining ½ cup of mayonnaise, the sour cream, the juice from ½ of the lemon, the pickle relish, and the mustard.
5. Place the cooked crab cakes on a serving platter and serve with the remaining ½ lemon cut into wedges and the dipping sauce.

Blackened Catfish

Servings: 4

Cooking Time: 8 Minutes

Ingredients:

- 1 teaspoon paprika
- 1 teaspoon garlic powder
- 1 teaspoon onion powder
- 1 teaspoon ground dried thyme
- ½ teaspoon ground black pepper
- ⅛ teaspoon cayenne pepper
- ½ teaspoon dried oregano
- ⅛ teaspoon crushed red pepper flakes
- 1 pound catfish filets
- ½ teaspoon sea salt
- 2 tablespoons butter, melted
- 1 tablespoon extra-virgin olive oil
- 2 tablespoons chopped parsley
- 1 lemon, cut into wedges

Directions:

1. In a small bowl, stir together the paprika, garlic powder, onion powder, thyme, black pepper, cayenne pepper, oregano, and crushed red pepper flakes.
2. Pat the fish dry with paper towels. Season the filets with sea salt and then coat with the blackening seasoning.
3. In a small bowl, mix together the butter and olive oil and drizzle over the fish filets, flipping them to coat them fully.
4. Preheat the toaster oven to 350°F.
5. Place the fish in the air fryer oven and air-fry for 8 minutes, checking the fish for doneness after 4 minutes. The fish will flake easily when cooked.
6. Remove the fish from the air fryer oven. Top with chopped parsley and serve with lemon wedges.

BEEF PORK AND LAMB

Spanish Pork Skewers

Servings: 4

Cooking Time: 16 Minutes

Ingredients:

- 1 pound pork tenderloin, cut into ¾- to 1-inch cubes
- 2 tablespoons olive oil
- 1 teaspoon ground cumin
- ½ teaspoon smoked paprika
- ½ teaspoon dried thyme leaves
- ½ teaspoon kosher salt, plus more for seasoning
- ⅛ teaspoon red pepper flakes
- 2 cloves garlic, minced
- 1 red bell pepper, cut into ¾- to 1-inch squares
- 1 small red onion, cut into ¾- to 1-inch wedges
- Freshly ground black pepper
- Nonstick cooking spray
- 2 tablespoons unsalted butter
- 1 tablespoon sherry or balsamic vinegar
- 1 teaspoon packed dark brown sugar

Directions:

1. Place the pork cubes in a medium bowl. Drizzle 1 tablespoon of oil over the pork. Stir the cumin, paprika, thyme, ½ teaspoon salt, the pepper flakes, and garlic in a small bowl. Sprinkle the seasonings over the pork. Stir to coat the pork evenly. Cover and refrigerate for at least 4 hours or up to overnight.
2. Place the bell pepper and onion pieces in a medium bowl. Drizzle with the remaining tablespoon olive oil and season with salt and pepper. Toss to coat evenly.
3. Alternately thread the pork and vegetables onto skewers. Spray a 12 x 12-inch baking pan with nonstick cooking spray. Place the filled skewers on the prepared pan. Place the pan in the toaster oven, positioning the skewers about 3 to 4 inches below the heating element. (Depending on your oven, you may need to set the rack to the middle position.)
4. Set the toaster oven on broil. Broil for 10 minutes. Turn the skewers. Broil for an additional 5 minutes, or until the vegetables are tender and a meat thermometer registers 145°F. Do not overcook.
5. Meanwhile, combine the butter, vinegar, and brown sugar in a small, glass, microwave-safe bowl. Season with salt and pepper. Microwave on High (100 percent) power for 45 seconds or until the butter melts and the mixture begins to bubble. Stir to dissolve the sugar.
6. Lightly brush the vinegar mixture over the skewers. Broil for 1 minute or until the skewers are browned.

Seasoned Boneless Pork Sirloin Chops

Servings: 2

Cooking Time: 16 Minutes

Ingredients:

- Seasoning mixture:
- ½ teaspoon ground cumin
- ¼ teaspoon turmeric
- Pinch of ground cardamom
- Pinch of grated nutmeg

- 1 teaspoon vegetable oil
- 1 teaspoon Pickapeppa sauce
- 2½- to ¾-pound boneless lean pork sirloin chops

Directions:

1. Combine the seasoning mixture ingredients in a small bowl and brush on both sides of the chops. Place the chops on the broiling rack with a pan underneath.
2. BROIL 8 minutes, remove the chops, turn, and brush with the mixture. Broil again for 8 minutes, or until the chops are done to your preference.

Easy Tex-mex Chimichangas

Servings: 2

Cooking Time: 8 Minutes

Ingredients:

- ¼ pound Thinly sliced deli roast beef, chopped
- ½ cup (about 2 ounces) Shredded Cheddar cheese or shredded Tex-Mex cheese blend
- ¼ cup Jarred salsa verde or salsa rojo
- ½ teaspoon Ground cumin
- ½ teaspoon Dried oregano
- 2 Burrito-size (12-inch) flour tortilla(s), not corn tortillas (gluten-free, if a concern)
- ⅔ cup Canned refried beans
- Vegetable oil spray

Directions:

1. Preheat the toaster oven to 375°F .
2. Stir the roast beef, cheese, salsa, cumin, and oregano in a bowl until well mixed.
3. Lay a tortilla on a clean, dry work surface. Spread ⅓ cup of the refried beans in the center lower third of the tortilla(s), leaving an inch on either side of the spread beans.
4. For one chimichanga, spread all of the roast beef mixture on top of the beans. For two, spread half of the roast beef mixture on each tortilla.
5. At either "end" of the filling mixture, fold the sides of the tortilla up and over the filling, partially covering it. Starting with the unfolded side of the tortilla just below the filling, roll the tortilla closed. Fold and roll the second filled tortilla, as necessary.
6. Coat the exterior of the tortilla(s) with vegetable oil spray. Set the chimichanga(s) seam side down in the air fryer oven, with at least ½ inch air space between them if you're working with two. Air-fry undisturbed for 8 minutes, or until the tortilla is lightly browned and crisp.
7. Use kitchen tongs to gently transfer the chimichanga(s) to a wire rack. Cool for at last 5 minutes or up to 20 minutes before serving.

Almond And Sun-dried Tomato Crusted Pork Chops

Servings: 4

Cooking Time: 10 Minutes

Ingredients:

- ½ cup oil-packed sun-dried tomatoes
- ½ cup toasted almonds
- ¼ cup grated Parmesan cheese
- ½ cup olive oil
- 2 tablespoons water
- ½ teaspoon salt
- freshly ground black pepper
- 4 center-cut boneless pork chops (about 1¼ pounds)

Directions:

1. Place the sun-dried tomatoes into a food processor and pulse them until they are coarsely chopped. Add the almonds, Parmesan cheese,

olive oil, water, salt and pepper. Process all the ingredients into a smooth paste. Spread most of the paste (leave a little in reserve) onto both sides of the pork chops and then pierce the meat several times with a needle-style meat tenderizer or a fork. Let the pork chops sit and marinate for at least 1 hour (refrigerate if marinating for longer than 1 hour).

2. Preheat the toaster oven to 370°F.
3. Brush a little olive oil on the bottom of the air fryer oven. Transfer the pork chops into the air fryer oven, spooning a little more of the sun-dried tomato paste onto the pork chops if there are any gaps where the paste may have been rubbed off. Air-fry the pork chops at 370°F for 10 minutes, turning the chops over halfway through the cooking process.
4. When the pork chops have finished cooking, transfer them to a serving plate and serve with mashed potatoes and vegetables for a hearty meal.

Meatloaf With Tangy Tomato Glaze

Servings: 6

Cooking Time: 50 Minutes

Ingredients:

- 1 pound ground beef
- ½ pound ground pork
- ½ pound ground veal (or turkey)
- 1 medium onion, diced
- 1 small clove of garlic, minced
- 2 egg yolks, lightly beaten
- ½ cup tomato ketchup
- 1 tablespoon Worcestershire sauce
- ½ cup plain breadcrumbs
- 2 teaspoons salt
- freshly ground black pepper
- ½ cup chopped fresh parsley, plus more for garnish
- 6 tablespoons ketchup
- 1 tablespoon balsamic vinegar
- 2 tablespoons brown sugar

Directions:

1. Combine the meats, onion, garlic, egg yolks, ketchup, Worcestershire sauce, breadcrumbs, salt, pepper and fresh parsley in a large bowl and mix well.
2. Preheat the toaster oven to 350°F and pour a little water into the bottom of the air fryer oven. (This will help prevent the grease that drips into the bottom drawer from burning and smoking.)
3. Transfer the meatloaf mixture to the air fryer oven, packing it down gently. Run a spatula around the meatloaf to create a space about ½-inch wide between the meat and the side of the air fryer oven.
4. Air-fry at 350°F for 20 minutes. Carefully invert the meatloaf onto a plate (remember to remove the pan from the air fryer oven so you don't pour all the grease out) and slide it back into the air fryer oven to turn it over. Re-shape the meatloaf with a spatula if necessary. Air-fry for another 20 minutes at 350°F.
5. Combine the ketchup, balsamic vinegar and brown sugar in a bowl and spread the mixture over the meatloaf. Air-fry for another 10 minutes, until an instant read thermometer inserted into the center of the meatloaf registers 160°F.
6. Allow the meatloaf to rest for a few more minutes and then transfer it to a serving platter using a spatula. Slice the meatloaf, sprinkle a little chopped parsley on top if desired, and serve.

Tuscan Pork Tenderloin

Servings: 4

Cooking Time: 35 Minutes

Ingredients:

- Nonstick cooking spray.
- 1 pork tenderloin (1 ¼ to 1 ½ pounds)
- Kosher salt and freshly ground black pepper
- 8 to 10 fresh basil leaves
- 1 ½ teaspoons minced garlic (about 3 cloves garlic)
- 2 slices prosciutto
- 2 ounces mozzarella cheese, cut into thin strips, or ½ cup shredded
- 1 tablespoon olive oil
- 1 teaspoon Italian seasoning

Directions:

1. Preheat the toaster oven to 400°F. Spray a 12 x 12-inch baking pan with nonstick cooking spray.
2. Cut the pork tenderloin in half lengthwise, not quite cutting through one side, and gently open it (like a book) so it lays flat. Cover the meat with plastic wrap. Pound the meat with the flat side of a meat pounder until the meat is even and about ½ inch thick.
3. Season the cut side of the meat with salt and pepper. Arrange the basil leaves evenly over the meat, then sprinkle with 1 teaspoon of the minced garlic. Top with an even layer of prosciutto and cheese. Roll the meat from the longer side covering the cheese and other filling ingredients completely. Tie the meat shut with kitchen twine, taking care to keep the roll tight and the filling inside.
4. Rub the outside of the meat with the olive oil. Mix the Italian seasoning and the remaining ½ teaspoon garlic in a small bowl. Season with salt and pepper. Rub the seasoning mixture evenly over the meat.
5. Place the meat in the prepared pan. Roast, uncovered, for 25 to 35 minutes or until the tenderloin is brown and the pork is just slightly pink inside.
6. Let stand for 5 to 10 minutes. Slice crosswise into slices about 1 inch thick.

Beef-stuffed Bell Peppers

Servings: 4

Cooking Time: 30 Minutes

Ingredients:

- 4 medium red or yellow bell peppers
- 1 pound extra-lean ground beef
- ½ sweet onion, finely chopped
- 2 teaspoons minced garlic
- 1 cup marinara sauce
- 1 cup ready-made brown or wild rice
- 1 cup fresh kale, chopped
- 1 teaspoon dried basil
- Sea salt, for seasoning
- Freshly ground black pepper, for seasoning
- 1 cup Swiss cheese, shredded

Directions:

1. Preheat the toaster oven to 350°F on AIR FRY for 5 minutes.
2. Cut the top off the peppers and scoop the seeds and membranes out. Set the pepper tops aside.
3. Place a large skillet over medium-high heat and brown the beef, about 10 minutes.
4. Add the onion and garlic and sauté until softened, about 4 minutes.
5. Add the marinara sauce, rice, kale, and basil, stirring to combine. Remove from the heat and season with salt and pepper.

6. Place the air-fryer basket in the baking tray and place the peppers in the basket, hollow-side up.

7. Evenly divide the filling among the peppers. You can place the pepper tops cut-side up and place the pepper bottoms in the tops to balance them, so that they do not tip over.

8. In position 1, air fry for 15 minutes until the peppers are tender. Top with the cheese and air fry for 2 more minutes more to melt the cheese. Serve.

Beef Vegetable Stew

Servings: 4

Cooking Time: 120 Minutes

Ingredients:

- 1 pound lean stewing beef, cut into 1-inch chunks
- 2 carrots, diced
- 2 celery stalks
- 1 large potato, diced
- ½ sweet onion, chopped
- 2 teaspoons minced garlic
- 1 (15-ounce) can diced tomatoes, with juices
- 1 teaspoon sea salt
- ½ teaspoon freshly ground black pepper
- 1 cup low-sodium beef broth
- 3 tablespoons all-purpose flour
- 1 cup frozen peas

Directions:

1. Place the rack in position 1 and preheat the toaster oven to 375°F on BAKE for 5 minutes.

2. In a 1½-quart casserole dish, combine the beef, carrots, celery, potato, onion, garlic, tomatoes, salt, and pepper.

3. In a small bowl, stir the broth and flour until well combined. Add the broth mixture to the beef mixture and stir to combine.

4. Cover with foil or a lid and bake for 2 hours, stirring each time you reset the timer, until the meat is very tender.

5. Stir in the peas and let stand for 10 minutes. Serve.

Steak With Herbed Butter

Servings: 2

Cooking Time: 16 Minutes

Ingredients:

- 4 tablespoons unsalted butter, softened
- 1 tablespoon minced flat-leaf (Italian) parsley
- 1 tablespoon chopped fresh chives
- 2 cloves garlic, minced
- 1 teaspoon Worcestershire sauce
- 2 beef strip steaks, cut about 1 ½ inches thick
- 1 tablespoon olive oil
- Kosher salt and freshly ground black pepper

Directions:

1. Combine the butter, parsley, chives, garlic, and Worcestershire sauce in a small bowl until well blended; set aside.

2. Preheat the toaster oven to broil.

3. Brush the steaks with olive oil and season with salt and pepper. Place the steak on the broiler rack set over the broiler pan. Place the pan in the toaster oven, positioning the steaks about 3 to 4 inches below the heating element. (Depending on your oven and the thickness of the steak, you may need to set the rack to the middle position.) Broil for 6 minutes, turn the steaks over, and broil for an additional 7 minutes. If necessary to reach the desired doneness, turn

the steaks over again and broil for an additional 3 minutes or until you reach your desired doneness.

4. Spread the herb butter generously over the steaks. Allow the steaks to stand for 5 to 10 minutes before slicing and serving.

Smokehouse-style Beef Ribs

Servings: 3

Cooking Time: 25 Minutes

Ingredients:

- ¼ teaspoon Mild smoked paprika
- ¼ teaspoon Garlic powder
- ¼ teaspoon Onion powder
- ¼ teaspoon Table salt
- ¼ teaspoon Ground black pepper
- 3 10- to 12-ounce beef back ribs (not beef short ribs)

Directions:

1. Preheat the toaster oven to 350°F .
2. Mix the smoked paprika, garlic powder, onion powder, salt, and pepper in a small bowl until uniform. Massage and pat this mixture onto the ribs.
3. When the machine is at temperature, set the ribs in the air fryer oven in one layer, turning them on their sides if necessary, sort of like they're spooning but with at least ¼ inch air space between them. Air-fry for 25 minutes, turning once, until deep brown and sizzling.
4. Use kitchen tongs to transfer the ribs to a wire rack. Cool for 5 minutes before serving.

Stuffed Pork Chops

Servings: 4

Cooking Time: 12 Minutes

Ingredients:

- 4 boneless pork chops
- ½ teaspoon salt
- ½ teaspoon black pepper
- ¼ teaspoon paprika
- 1 cup frozen spinach, defrosted and squeezed dry
- 2 cloves garlic, minced
- 2 ounces cream cheese
- ¼ cup grated Parmesan cheese
- 1 tablespoon extra-virgin olive oil

Directions:

1. Pat the pork chops with a paper towel. Make a slit in the side of each pork chop to create a pouch.
2. Season the pork chops with the salt, pepper, and paprika.
3. In a small bowl, mix together the spinach, garlic, cream cheese, and Parmesan cheese.
4. Divide the mixture into fourths and stuff the pork chop pouches. Secure the pouches with toothpicks.
5. Preheat the toaster oven to 400°F.
6. Place the stuffed pork chops in the air fryer oven and spray liberally with cooking spray. Air-fry for 6 minutes, flip and coat with more cooking spray, and cook another 6 minutes. Check to make sure the meat is cooked to an internal temperature of 145°F. Cook the pork chops in batches, as needed.

Barbecued Broiled Pork Chops

Servings: 2

Cooking Time: 16 Minutes

Ingredients:

- Barbecue sauce mixture:
- 1 tablespoon ketchup
- ¼ cup dry red wine
- 1 tablespoon vegetable oil

- ⅛ teaspoon smoked flavoring (liquid smoke)
- 1 teaspoon chili powder
- 1 teaspoon ground cumin
- 1 teaspoon brown sugar
- ¼ teaspoon butcher's pepper
- 2 large (6- to 8-ounce) lean pork chops, approximately ¾ to 1 inch thick

Directions:

1. Combine the barbecue sauce mixture ingredients in a small bowl. Brush the chops with the sauce and place on a broiling rack with a pan underneath.
2. BROIL 8 minutes, turn with tongs, and broil for another 8 minutes, or until the meat is cooked to your preference.

Kielbasa Sausage With Pierogies And Caramelized Onions

Servings: 3

Cooking Time: 30 Minutes

Ingredients:

- 1 Vidalia or sweet onion, sliced
- olive oil
- salt and freshly ground black pepper
- 2 tablespoons butter, cut into small cubes
- 1 teaspoon sugar
- 1 pound light Polish kielbasa sausage, cut into 2-inch chunks
- 1 (13-ounce) package frozen mini pierogies
- 2 teaspoons vegetable or olive oil
- chopped scallions

Directions:

1. Preheat the toaster oven to 400°F.
2. Toss the sliced onions with a little olive oil, salt and pepper and transfer them to the air fryer oven. Dot the onions with pieces of butter and air-fry at 400°F for 2 minutes. Then sprinkle the sugar over the onions and stir. Pour any melted butter from the bottom of the air fryer oven over the onions (do this over the sink – some of the butter will spill through the pan). Continue to air-fry for another 13 minutes, stirring the pan every few minutes to cook the onions evenly.
3. Add the kielbasa chunks to the onions and toss. Air-fry for another 5 minutes. Transfer the kielbasa and onions to a bowl and cover with aluminum foil to keep warm.
4. Toss the frozen pierogies with the vegetable or olive oil and transfer them to the air fryer oven. Air-fry at 400°F for 8 minutes.
5. When the pierogies have finished cooking, return the kielbasa and onions to the air fryer oven and gently toss with the pierogies. Air-fry for 2 more minutes and then transfer everything to a serving platter. Garnish with the chopped scallions and serve hot with the spicy sour cream sauce below.
6. Kielbasa Sausage with Pierogies and Caramelized Onions

California Burritos

Servings: 4

Cooking Time: 17 Minutes

Ingredients:

- 1 pound sirloin steak, sliced thin
- 1 teaspoon dried oregano
- 1 teaspoon ground cumin
- ½ teaspoon garlic powder
- 16 tater tots
- ⅓ cup sour cream
- ½ lime, juiced
- 2 tablespoons hot sauce
- 1 large avocado, pitted

- 1 teaspoon salt, divided
- 4 large (8- to 10-inch) flour tortillas
- ½ cup shredded cheddar cheese or Monterey jack
- 2 tablespoons avocado oil

Directions:

1. Preheat the toaster oven to 380°F.
2. Season the steak with oregano, cumin, and garlic powder. Place the steak on one side of the air fryer oven and the tater tots on the other side. (It's okay for them to touch, because the flavors will all come together in the burrito.) Air-fry for 8 minutes, toss, and cook an additional 4 to 6 minutes.
3. Meanwhile, in a small bowl, stir together the sour cream, lime juice, and hot sauce.
4. In another small bowl, mash together the avocado and season with ½ teaspoon of the salt, to taste.
5. To assemble the burrito, lay out the tortillas, equally divide the meat amongst the tortillas. Season the steak equally with the remaining ½ teaspoon salt. Then layer the mashed avocado and sour cream mixture on top. Top each tortilla with 4 tater tots and finish each with 2 tablespoons cheese. Roll up the sides and, while holding in the sides, roll up the burrito. Place the burritos in the air fryer oven and brush with avocado oil (working in batches as needed); air-fry for 3 minutes or until lightly golden on the outside.

Calf's Liver

Servings: 4

Cooking Time: 5 Minutes

Ingredients:

- 1 pound sliced calf's liver
- salt and pepper
- 2 eggs
- 2 tablespoons milk
- ½ cup whole wheat flour
- 1½ cups panko breadcrumbs
- ½ cup plain breadcrumbs
- ½ teaspoon salt
- ¼ teaspoon pepper
- oil for misting or cooking spray

Directions:

1. Cut liver slices crosswise into strips about ½-inch wide. Sprinkle with salt and pepper to taste.
2. Beat together egg and milk in a shallow dish.
3. Place wheat flour in a second shallow dish.
4. In a third shallow dish, mix together panko, plain breadcrumbs, ½ teaspoon salt, and ¼ teaspoon pepper.
5. Preheat the toaster oven to 390°F.
6. Dip liver strips in flour, egg wash, and then breadcrumbs, pressing in coating slightly to make crumbs stick.
7. Cooking half the liver at a time, place strips in air fryer oven in a single layer, close but not touching. Air-fry at 390°F for 5 minutes or until done to your preference.
8. Repeat step 7 to cook remaining liver.

Spicy Little Beef Birds

Servings: 2

Cooking Time: 12 Minutes

Ingredients:

- Spicy mixture:
- 1 tablespoon olive oil
- 1 tablespoon brown mustard
- 1 teaspoon chili powder
- 1 teaspoon garlic powder
- 1 teaspoon hot sauce
- 1 tablespoon barbecue sauce or salsa

- Salt and freshly ground black pepper to taste
- ½ to ¾ pound pepper steaks, cut into 3 × 4-inch strips

Directions:

1. Blend the spicy mixture ingredients in a small bowl and brush both sides of the beef strips.
2. Roll up the strips lengthwise and fasten with toothpicks near each end. Place the beef rolls in an oiled or nonstick 8½ × 8½ × 2-inch square baking (cake) pan.
3. BROIL for 6 minutes, remove from the oven, and turn with tongs. Brush with the spicy mixture and broil again for 6 minutes, or until done to your preference.

Pretzel-coated Pork Tenderloin

Servings: 4

Cooking Time: 10 Minutes

Ingredients:

- 1 Large egg white(s)
- 2 teaspoons Dijon mustard (gluten-free, if a concern)
- 1½ cups (about 6 ounces) Crushed pretzel crumbs
- 1 pound (4 sections) Pork tenderloin, cut into ¼-pound (4-ounce) sections
- Vegetable oil spray

Directions:

1. Preheat the toaster oven to 350°F .
2. Set up and fill two shallow soup plates or small pie plates on your counter: one for the egg white(s), whisked with the mustard until foamy; and one for the pretzel crumbs.
3. Dip a section of pork tenderloin in the egg white mixture and turn it to coat well, even on the ends. Let any excess egg white mixture slip back into the rest, then set the pork in the pretzel crumbs. Roll it several times, pressing gently, until the pork is evenly coated, even on the ends. Generously coat the pork section with vegetable oil spray, set it aside, and continue coating and spraying the remaining sections.
4. Set the pork sections in the air fryer oven with at least ¼ inch between them. Air-fry undisturbed for 10 minutes, or until an instant-read meat thermometer inserted into the center of one section registers 145°F.
5. Use kitchen tongs to transfer the pieces to a wire rack. Cool for 3 to 5 minutes before serving.

Stuffed Bell Peppers

Servings: 4

Cooking Time: 10 Minutes

Ingredients:

- ¼ pound lean ground pork
- ¾ pound lean ground beef
- ¼ cup onion, minced
- 1 15-ounce can Red Gold crushed tomatoes
- 1 teaspoon Worcestershire sauce
- 1 teaspoon barbeque seasoning
- 1 teaspoon honey
- ½ teaspoon dried basil
- ½ cup cooked brown rice
- ½ teaspoon garlic powder
- ½ teaspoon oregano
- ½ teaspoon salt
- 2 small bell peppers

Directions:

1. Place pork, beef, and onion in air fryer oven baking pan and air-fry at 360°F for 5 minutes.
2. Stir to break apart chunks and cook 3 more minutes. Continue cooking and stirring in 2-minute intervals until meat is well done. Remove from pan and drain.

3. In a small saucepan, combine the tomatoes, Worcestershire, barbeque seasoning, honey, and basil. Stir well to mix in honey and seasonings.
4. In a large bowl, combine the cooked meat mixture, rice, garlic powder, oregano, and salt. Add ¼ cup of the seasoned crushed tomatoes. Stir until well mixed.
5. Cut peppers in half and remove stems and seeds.
6. Stuff each pepper half with one fourth of the meat mixture.
7. Place the peppers in air fryer oven and air-fry for 10 minutes, until peppers are crisp tender.
8. Heat remaining tomato sauce. Serve peppers with warm sauce spooned over top.

Crispy Lamb Shoulder Chops

Servings: 3
Cooking Time: 28 Minutes

Ingredients:

- ¾ cup All-purpose flour or gluten-free all-purpose flour
- 2 teaspoons Mild paprika
- 2 teaspoons Table salt
- 1½ teaspoons Garlic powder
- 1½ teaspoons Dried sage leaves
- 3 6-ounce bone-in lamb shoulder chops, any excess fat trimmed
- Olive oil spray

Directions:

1. Whisk the flour, paprika, salt, garlic powder, and sage in a large bowl until the mixture is of a uniform color. Add the chops and toss well to coat. Transfer them to a cutting board.
2. Preheat the toaster oven to 375°F .
3. When the machine is at temperature, again dredge the chops one by one in the flour mixture. Lightly coat both sides of each chop with olive oil spray before putting it in the air fryer oven. Continue on with the remaining chop(s), leaving air space between them in the air fryer oven.
4. Air-fry, turning once, for 25 minutes, or until the chops are well browned and tender when pierced with the point of a paring knife. If the machine is at 360°F, you may need to add up to 3 minutes to the cooking time.
5. Use kitchen tongs to transfer the chops to a wire rack. Cool for 5 minutes before serving.

Kielbasa Chunks With Pineapple & Peppers

Servings: 2
Cooking Time: 10 Minutes

Ingredients:

- ¾ pound kielbasa sausage
- 1 cup bell pepper chunks (any color)
- 1 8-ounce can pineapple chunks in juice, drained
- 1 tablespoon barbeque seasoning
- 1 tablespoon soy sauce
- cooking spray

Directions:

1. Cut sausage into ½-inch slices.
2. In a medium bowl, toss all ingredients together.
3. Spray air fryer oven with nonstick cooking spray.
4. Pour sausage mixture into the air fryer oven.
5. Air-fry at 390°F for approximately 5 minutes. Cook an additional 5 minutes.

Glazed Meatloaf

Servings: 4

Cooking Time: 60 Minutes

Ingredients:

- 2 pounds extra-lean ground beef
- ½ cup fine bread crumbs
- 1 large egg
- 1 medium carrot, shredded
- 2 teaspoons minced garlic
- ¼ cup milk
- 1 tablespoon Italian seasoning
- ½ teaspoon sea salt
- ⅛ teaspoon freshly ground black pepper
- ½ cup ketchup
- 1 tablespoon dark brown sugar
- 1 teaspoon apple cider vinegar

Directions:

1. Place the rack in position 1 and preheat the toaster oven to 375°F on BAKE for 5 minutes.
2. In a large bowl, mix the ground beef, bread crumbs, egg, carrot, garlic, milk, Italian seasoning, salt, and pepper until well combined.
3. Press the mixture into a 9-by-5-inch loaf pan.
4. In a small bowl, stir the ketchup, brown sugar, and vinegar. Set aside.
5. Bake for 40 minutes.
6. Take the meatloaf out and spread the glaze over the top. Bake an additional 20 minutes until cooked through, with an internal temperature of 165°F. Serve.

Minted Lamb Chops

Servings: 4

Cooking Time: 15 Minutes

Ingredients:

- Mint mixture:
- 4 tablespoons finely chopped fresh mint
- 2 tablespoons nonfat yogurt
- 1 tablespoon olive oil
- Salt and freshly ground black pepper to taste
- 4 lean lamb chops, fat trimmed, approximately ¾ inch thick
- 1 tablespoon balsamic vinegar

Directions:

1. Combine the mint mixture ingredients in a small bowl, stirring well to blend. Set aside. Place the lamp chops on a broiling rack with a pan underneath.
2. BROIL the lamb chops for 10 minutes, or until they are slightly pink. Remove from the oven and brush one side liberally with balsamic vinegar. Turn the chops over with tongs and spread with the mint mixture, using all of the mixture.
3. BROIL again for 5 minutes, or until lightly browned.

Mustard-herb Lamb Chops

Servings: 2

Cooking Time: 15 Minutes

Ingredients:

- 2 tablespoons Dijon mustard
- 1 teaspoon minced garlic
- ¼ cup bread crumbs
- 1 teaspoon dried Italian herbs
- Zest of 1 lemon
- 4 lamb loin chops (about 1 pound), room temperature
- Sea salt, for seasoning
- Freshly ground black pepper, for seasoning
- Oil spray (hand-pumped)

Directions:

1. Preheat the toaster oven to 425°F on CONVECTION BAKE for 5 minutes.
2. Line the baking tray with parchment or aluminum foil.
3. In a small bowl, stir the mustard and garlic until blended.
4. In another small bowl, stir the bread crumbs, herbs, and lemon zest until mixed.
5. Lightly season the lamb chops on both sides with salt and pepper. Brush the mustard mixture over a chop and dredge it in the bread crumb mixture to lightly bread the lamb. Set the lamb on the baking tray and repeat with the other chops.
6. Spray the chops lightly with the oil, and in position 2, bake for 15 minutes until browned and the internal temperature is 130°F for medium-rare.
7. Rest the lamb for 5 minutes, then serve.

Pork Taco Gorditas

Servings: 4
Cooking Time: 21 Minutes

Ingredients:

- 1 pound lean ground pork
- 2 tablespoons chili powder
- 2 tablespoons ground cumin
- 1 teaspoon dried oregano
- 2 teaspoons paprika
- 1 teaspoon garlic powder
- ½ cup water
- 1 (15-ounce) can pinto beans, drained and rinsed
- ½ cup taco sauce
- salt and freshly ground black pepper
- 2 cups grated Cheddar cheese
- 5 (12-inch) flour tortillas
- 4 (8-inch) crispy corn tortilla shells
- 4 cups shredded lettuce
- 1 tomato, diced
- ⅓ cup sliced black olives
- sour cream, for serving
- tomato salsa, for serving

Directions:

1. Preheat the toaster oven to 400°F.
2. Place the ground pork in the air fryer oven and air-fry at 400°F for 10 minutes, stirring a few times during the cooking process to gently break up the meat. Combine the chili powder, cumin, oregano, paprika, garlic powder and water in a small bowl. Stir the spice mixture into the browned pork. Stir in the beans and taco sauce and air-fry for an additional minute. Transfer the pork mixture to a bowl. Season to taste with salt and freshly ground black pepper.
3. Sprinkle ½ cup of the shredded cheese in the center of four of the flour tortillas, making sure to leave a 2-inch border around the edge free of cheese and filling. Divide the pork mixture among the four tortillas, placing it on top of the cheese. Place a crunchy corn tortilla on top of the pork and top with shredded lettuce, diced tomatoes, and black olives. Cut the remaining flour tortilla into 4 quarters. These quarters of tortilla will serve as the bottom of the gordita. Place one quarter tortilla on top of each gordita and fold the edges of the bottom flour tortilla up over the sides, enclosing the filling. While holding the seams down, brush the bottom of the gordita with olive oil and place the seam side down on the countertop while you finish the remaining three gorditas.
4. Preheat the toaster oven to 380°F.

5. Air-fry one gordita at a time. Transfer the gordita carefully to the air fryer oven, seam side down. Brush or spray the top tortilla with oil and air-fry for 5 minutes. Carefully turn the gordita over and air-fry for an additional 5 minutes, until both sides are browned. When finished air frying all four gorditas, layer them back into the air fryer oven for an additional minute to make sure they are all warm before serving with sour cream and salsa.

Lamb Burger With Feta And Olives

Servings: 3
Cooking Time: 16 Minutes

Ingredients:

- 2 teaspoons olive oil
- ⅓ onion, finely chopped
- 1 clove garlic, minced
- 1 pound ground lamb
- 2 tablespoons fresh parsley, finely chopped
- 1½ teaspoons fresh oregano, finely chopped
- ½ cup black olives, finely chopped
- ⅓ cup crumbled feta cheese
- ½ teaspoon salt
- freshly ground black pepper
- 4 thick pita breads
- toppings and condiments

Directions:

1. Preheat a medium skillet over medium-high heat on the stovetop. Add the olive oil and cook the onion until tender, but not browned – about 4 to 5 minutes. Add the garlic and air-fry for another minute. Transfer the onion and garlic to a mixing bowl and add the ground lamb, parsley, oregano, olives, feta cheese, salt and pepper. Gently mix the ingredients together.
2. Divide the mixture into 3 or 4 equal portions and then form the hamburgers, being careful not to over-handle the meat. One good way to do this is to throw the meat back and forth between your hands like a baseball, packing the meat each time you catch it. Flatten the balls into patties, making an indentation in the center of each patty. Flatten the sides of the patties as well to make it easier to fit them into the air fryer oven.
3. Preheat the toaster oven to 370°F.
4. If you don't have room for all four burgers, air-fry two or three burgers at a time for 8 minutes at 370°F. Flip the burgers over and air-fry for another 8 minutes. If you cooked your burgers in batches, return the first batch of burgers to the air fryer oven for the last two minutes of cooking to re-heat. This should give you a medium-well burger. If you'd prefer a medium-rare burger, shorten the cooking time to about 13 minutes. Remove the burgers to a resting plate and let the burgers rest for a few minutes before dressing and serving.
5. While the burgers are resting, toast the pita breads in the air fryer oven for 2 minutes. Tuck the burgers into the toasted pita breads, or wrap the pitas around the burgers and serve with a tzatziki sauce or some mayonnaise.

Orange Glazed Pork Tenderloin

Servings: 3
Cooking Time: 23 Minutes

Ingredients:

- 2 tablespoons brown sugar
- 2 teaspoons cornstarch
- 2 teaspoons Dijon mustard
- ½ cup orange juice
- ½ teaspoon soy sauce

- 2 teaspoons grated fresh ginger
- ¼ cup white wine
- zest of 1 orange
- 1 pound pork tenderloin
- salt and freshly ground black pepper
- oranges, halved (for garnish)
- fresh parsley or other green herb (for garnish)

Directions:

1. Combine the brown sugar, cornstarch, Dijon mustard, orange juice, soy sauce, ginger, white wine and orange zest in a small saucepan and bring the mixture to a boil on the stovetop. Lower the heat and simmer while you cook the pork tenderloin or until the sauce has thickened.
2. Preheat the toaster oven to 370°F.
3. Season all sides of the pork tenderloin with salt and freshly ground black pepper. Transfer the tenderloin to the air fryer oven, bending the pork into a wide "U" shape if necessary to fit in the air fryer oven. Air-fry at 370°F for 20 to 23 minutes, or until the internal temperature reaches 145°F. Flip the tenderloin over halfway through the cooking process and baste with the sauce.
4. Transfer the tenderloin to a cutting board and let it rest for 5 minutes. Slice the pork at a slight angle and serve immediately with orange halves and fresh herbs to dress it up. Drizzle any remaining glaze over the top.

Barbeque Ribs

Servings: 4

Cooking Time: 35 Minutes

Ingredients:

- 2 pounds pork spareribs or baby back ribs, silver skin removed
- 2 tablespoons brown sugar
- 1 teaspoon chili powder
- 1 teaspoon dry mustard
- Sea salt, for seasoning
- Freshly ground black pepper, for seasoning
- Oil spray (hand-pumped)
- 1 cup barbeque sauce

Directions:

1. Preheat the toaster oven to 375°F on AIR FRY for 5 minutes.
2. Cut the ribs into 4 bone sections or to fit in the basket.
3. In a small bowl, combine the brown sugar, chili powder, and mustard, and rub it all over the ribs.
4. Season the ribs with salt and pepper.
5. Place the air-fryer basket in the baking tray and spray it generously with the oil.
6. Arrange the ribs in the basket. There can be overlap if necessary.
7. In position 2, air fry for 35 minutes, turning halfway through, until the ribs are tender, browned, and crisp.
8. Baste the ribs with the barbeque sauce and serve.

Sloppy Joes

Servings: 4

Cooking Time: 17 Minutes

Ingredients:

- oil for misting or cooking spray
- 1 pound very lean ground beef
- 1 teaspoon onion powder
- ⅓ cup ketchup
- ¼ cup water
- ½ teaspoon celery seed
- 1 tablespoon lemon juice
- 1½ teaspoons brown sugar

- 1¼ teaspoons low-sodium Worcestershire sauce
- ½ teaspoon salt (optional)
- ½ teaspoon vinegar
- ⅛ teaspoon dry mustard
- hamburger or slider buns

Directions:

1. Spray air fryer oven with nonstick cooking spray or olive oil.
2. Break raw ground beef into small chunks and pile into air fryer oven.
3. Air-fry at 390°F for 5 minutes. Stir to break apart and cook 3 minutes. Stir and cook 4 minutes longer or until meat is well done.
4. Remove meat from air fryer oven, drain, and use a knife and fork to crumble into small pieces.
5. Give your air fryer oven a quick rinse to remove any bits of meat.
6. Place all the remaining ingredients except the buns in a 6 x 6-inch baking pan and mix together.
7. Add meat and stir well.
8. Air-fry at 330°F for 5 minutes. Stir and air-fry for 2 minutes.
9. Scoop onto buns.

POULTRY

East Indian Chicken

Servings: 4

Cooking Time: 45 Minutes

Ingredients:

- Sauce mixture:
- ¼ cup white wine
- ¼ cup red wine
- ½ cup low-sodium vegetable broth
- ½ cup finely chopped onion
- ½ cup finely chopped bell pepper
- ½ cup finely chopped fresh tomato
- 3 garlic cloves, minced
- 1 tablespoon peeled and minced fresh ginger
- 2 teaspoons curry powder
- ¼ teaspoon ground cinnamon
- ¼ teaspoon ground cumin
- 4 small dried chilies
- Salt and freshly ground black pepper to taste
- 6 skinless, boneless chicken thighs

Directions:

1. Preheat the toaster oven to 400° F.
2. Combine the sauce mixture ingredients in a 1-quart 8½ × 8½ × 4-inch ovenproof baking dish and mix well. Add the chicken and toss together to coat well. Cover the dish with aluminum foil.
3. BAKE for 45 minutes, or until the chicken is tender. Uncover and spoon the sauce over the chicken. Remove the chilies before serving.

Crispy Fried Onion Chicken Breasts

Servings: 2

Cooking Time: 13 Minutes

Ingredients:

- ¼ cup all-purpose flour
- salt and freshly ground black pepper
- 1 egg
- 2 tablespoons Dijon mustard
- 1½ cups crispy fried onions (like French's®)
- ½ teaspoon paprika
- 2 (5-ounce) boneless, skinless chicken breasts
- vegetable or olive oil, in a spray bottle

Directions:

1. Preheat the toaster oven to 380°F.
2. Set up a dredging station with three shallow dishes. Place the flour in the first shallow dish and season well with salt and freshly ground black pepper. Combine the egg and Dijon mustard in a second shallow dish and whisk until smooth. Place the fried onions in a sealed bag and using a rolling pin, crush them into coarse crumbs. Combine these crumbs with the paprika in the third shallow dish.
3. Dredge the chicken breasts in the flour. Shake off any excess flour and dip them into the egg mixture. Let any excess egg drip off. Then coat both sides of the chicken breasts with the crispy onions. Press the crumbs onto the chicken breasts with your hands to make sure they are well adhered.
4. Spray or brush the bottom of the air fryer oven with oil. Transfer the chicken breasts to the air fryer oven and air-fry at 380°F for 13 minutes, turning the chicken over halfway through the cooking time.
5. Serve immediately.

Honey Lemon Thyme Glazed Cornish Hen

Servings: 2

Cooking Time: 20 Minutes

Ingredients:

- 1 (2-pound) Cornish game hen, split in half
- olive oil
- salt and freshly ground black pepper
- ¼ teaspoon dried thyme
- ¼ cup honey
- 1 tablespoon lemon zest
- juice of 1 lemon
- 1½ teaspoons chopped fresh thyme leaves
- ½ teaspoon soy sauce
- freshly ground black pepper

Directions:

1. Split the game hen in half by cutting down each side of the backbone and then cutting through the breast. Brush or spray both halves of the game hen with the olive oil and then season with the salt, pepper and dried thyme.
2. Preheat the toaster oven to 390°F.
3. Place the game hen, skin side down, into the air fryer oven and air-fry for 5 minutes. Turn the hen halves over and air-fry for 10 minutes.
4. While the hen is cooking, combine the honey, lemon zest and juice, fresh thyme, soy sauce and pepper in a small bowl.
5. When the air fryer oven timer rings, brush the honey glaze onto the game hen and continue to air-fry for another 3 to 5 minutes, just until the hen is nicely glazed, browned and has an internal temperature of 165°F.
6. Let the hen rest for 5 minutes and serve warm.

Light And Lovely Loaf

Servings: 4

Cooking Time: 30 Minutes

Ingredients:

- 2 cups ground chicken or turkey breast
- 1 egg
- ½ cup grated carrot
- ½ cup grated celery
- 1 tablespoon finely chopped onion
- ½ teaspoon garlic powder
- Salt and freshly ground black pepper to taste

Directions:

1. Preheat the toaster oven to 400° F.
2. Blend all ingredients in a bowl, mixing well, and transfer to an oiled or nonstick regular-size 4½ × 8½ × 2¼-inch loaf pan
3. BAKE, uncovered, for 30 minutes, until lightly browned.

Mediterranean Stuffed Chicken Breasts

Servings: 4

Cooking Time: 24 Minutes

Ingredients:

- 4 boneless, skinless chicken breasts
- ½ teaspoon salt
- ½ teaspoon black pepper
- ½ teaspoon garlic powder
- ½ teaspoon paprika
- ½ cup canned artichoke hearts, chopped
- 4 ounces cream cheese
- ¼ cup grated Parmesan cheese

Directions:

1. Pat the chicken breasts with a paper towel. Using a sharp knife, cut a pouch in the side of each chicken breast for filling.

2. In a small bowl, mix the salt, pepper, garlic powder, and paprika. Season the chicken breasts with this mixture.
3. In a medium bowl, mix together the artichokes, cream cheese, and grated Parmesan cheese. Divide the filling between the 4 breasts, stuffing it inside the pouches. Use toothpicks to close the pouches and secure the filling.
4. Preheat the toaster oven to 360°F.
5. Spray the air fryer oven liberally with cooking spray, add the stuffed chicken breasts to the air fryer oven, and spray liberally with cooking spray again. Air-fry for 14 minutes, carefully turn over the chicken breasts, and cook another 10 minutes. Check the temperature at 20 minutes cooking. Chicken breasts are fully cooked when the center measures 165°F. Cook in batches, if needed.

Chicken Schnitzel Dogs

Servings: 4
Cooking Time: 10 Minutes

Ingredients:

- ½ cup flour
- ½ teaspoon salt
- 1 teaspoon marjoram
- 1 teaspoon dried parsley flakes
- ½ teaspoon thyme
- 1 egg
- 1 teaspoon lemon juice
- 1 teaspoon water
- 1 cup breadcrumbs
- 4 chicken tenders, pounded thin
- oil for misting or cooking spray
- 4 whole-grain hotdog buns
- 4 slices Gouda cheese
- 1 small Granny Smith apple, thinly sliced
- ½ cup shredded Napa cabbage
- coleslaw dressing

Directions:

1. In a shallow dish, mix together the flour, salt, marjoram, parsley, and thyme.
2. In another shallow dish, beat together egg, lemon juice, and water.
3. Place breadcrumbs in a third shallow dish.
4. Cut each of the flattened chicken tenders in half lengthwise.
5. Dip flattened chicken strips in flour mixture, then egg wash. Let excess egg drip off and roll in breadcrumbs. Spray both sides with oil or cooking spray.
6. Air-fry at 390°F for 5 minutes. Spray with oil, turn over, and spray other side.
7. Air-fry for 3 to 5 minutes more, until well done and crispy brown.
8. To serve, place 2 schnitzel strips on bottom of each hot dog bun. Top with cheese, sliced apple, and cabbage. Drizzle with coleslaw dressing and top with other half of bun.

Chicken Parmesan

Servings: 4
Cooking Time: 11 Minutes

Ingredients:

- 4 chicken tenders
- Italian seasoning
- salt
- ¼ cup cornstarch
- ½ cup Italian salad dressing
- ¼ cup panko breadcrumbs
- ¼ cup grated Parmesan cheese, plus more for serving
- oil for misting or cooking spray
- 8 ounces spaghetti, cooked
- 1 24-ounce jar marinara sauce

Directions:

1. Pound chicken tenders with meat mallet or rolling pin until about ¼-inch thick.
2. Sprinkle both sides with Italian seasoning and salt to taste.
3. Place cornstarch and salad dressing in 2 separate shallow dishes.
4. In a third shallow dish, mix together the panko crumbs and Parmesan cheese.
5. Dip flattened chicken in cornstarch, then salad dressing. Dip in the panko mixture, pressing into the chicken so the coating sticks well.
6. Spray both sides with oil or cooking spray. Place in air fryer oven in single layer.
7. Air-fry at 390°F for 5 minutes. Spray with oil again, turning chicken to coat both sides. See tip about turning.
8. Air-fry for an additional 6 minutes or until chicken juices run clear and outside is browned.
9. While chicken is cooking, heat marinara sauce and stir into cooked spaghetti.
10. To serve, divide spaghetti with sauce among 4 dinner plates, and top each with a fried chicken tender. Pass additional Parmesan at the table for those who want extra cheese.

Gluten-free Nutty Chicken Fingers

Servings: 4

Cooking Time: 10 Minutes

Ingredients:

- ½ cup gluten-free flour
- ½ teaspoon garlic powder
- ¼ teaspoon onion powder
- ¼ teaspoon black pepper
- ¼ teaspoon salt
- 1 cup walnuts, pulsed into coarse flour
- ½ cup gluten-free breadcrumbs
- 2 large eggs
- 1 pound boneless, skinless chicken tenders

Directions:

1. Preheat the toaster oven to 400°F.
2. In a medium bowl, mix the flour, garlic, onion, pepper, and salt. Set aside.
3. In a separate bowl, mix the walnut flour and breadcrumbs.
4. In a third bowl, whisk the eggs.
5. Liberally spray the air fryer oven with olive oil spray.
6. Pat the chicken tenders dry with a paper towel. Dredge the tenders one at a time in the flour, then dip them in the egg, and toss them in the breadcrumb coating. Repeat until all tenders are coated.
7. Set each tender in the air fryer oven, leaving room on each side of the tender to allow for flipping.
8. When the air fryer oven is full, cook 5 minutes, flip, and cook another 5 minutes. Check the internal temperature after cooking completes; it should read 165°F. If it does not, cook another 2 to 4 minutes.
9. Remove the tenders and let cool 5 minutes before serving. Repeat until all the tenders are cooked.

Tender Chicken Meatballs

Servings: 4

Cooking Time: 30 Minutes

Ingredients:

- 1 pound lean ground chicken
- ½ cup bread crumbs
- 1 large egg

- 1 scallion, both white and green parts, finely chopped
- ¼ cup whole milk
- ¼ cup shredded, unsweetened coconut
- 1 tablespoon low-sodium soy sauce
- 1 teaspoon minced garlic
- 1 teaspoon fresh ginger, peeled and grated
- Pinch cayenne powder
- Oil spray (hand-pumped)

Directions:

1. Preheat the toaster oven to 375°F on BAKE for 5 minutes.
2. Line the baking tray with parchment and set aside.
3. In a large bowl, mix the chicken, bread crumbs, egg, scallion, milk, coconut, soy sauce, garlic, ginger, and cayenne until very well combined.
4. Shape the chicken mixture into 1½-inch balls and place them in a single layer on the baking tray. Do not overcrowd them.
5. In position 2, bake for 20 minutes, turning halfway through, until they are cooked through and evenly browned. Serve.

Guiltless Bacon

Servings: 4

Cooking Time: 10 Minutes

Ingredients:

- 6 slices lean turkey bacon, placed on a broiling pan

Directions:

1. BROIL 5 minutes, turn the pieces, and broil again for 5 more minutes, or until done to your preference. Press the slices between paper towels and serve immediately.

I Forgot To Thaw—garlic Capered Chicken Thighs

Servings: 4

Cooking Time: 50 Minutes

Ingredients:

- 6 frozen skinless, boneless chicken thighs
- Garlic mixture:
- 3 garlic cloves, minced
- ¾ cup dry white wine
- 2 tablespoons capers
- ½ teaspoon paprika
- ¼ teaspoon ground cumin
- Salt and freshly ground black pepper to taste

Directions:

1. Preheat the toaster oven to 400° F.
2. Thaw the chicken as directed. Separate the pieces and add the garlic mixture, which has been combined in a small bowl, stirring well to coat. Cover the dish with aluminum foil.
3. BAKE for 30 minutes, or until the chicken is tender. Remove the cover and turn the chicken pieces, spooning the sauce over them.
4. BROIL for 8 minutes, or until the chicken is lightly browned.

Chicken Fajitas

Servings: 4

Cooking Time: 15 Minutes

Ingredients:

- FOR THE FAJITAS
- ½ teaspoon ground cumin
- ½ teaspoon garlic powder
- ¼ teaspoon smoked paprika
- ¼ teaspoon onion powder
- ¼ teaspoon chili powder

- 1 pound boneless, skinless chicken breast, cut into ¼-inch strips
- 1 red bell pepper, cut into thin slices
- 1 green bell pepper, cut into thin slices
- 1 small red onion, cut into thin slices
- 2 tablespoons olive oil
- 8 (6-inch) tortillas
- OPTIONAL TOPPINGS
- Salsa
- Sour cream
- Pickled jalapeños
- Shredded lettuce

Directions:

1. Preheat the toaster oven to 375°F on AIR FRY for 5 minutes.
2. Place the air-fryer basket in the baking tray.
3. In a large bowl, stir the cumin, garlic powder, paprika, onion powder, and chili powder until well mixed. Add the chicken, bell peppers, onion, and oil, and toss to coat evenly.
4. Spread the chicken and veggies on the baking sheet.
5. In position 2, air fry for 15 minutes, tossing them halfway through, until cooked and the vegetables are lightly browned.
6. Serve tucked into the tortillas with your favorite toppings.

Peanut Butter-barbeque Chicken

Servings: 4

Cooking Time: 20 Minutes

Ingredients:

- 1 pound boneless, skinless chicken thighs
- salt and pepper
- 1 large orange
- ½ cup barbeque sauce
- 2 tablespoons smooth peanut butter
- 2 tablespoons chopped peanuts for garnish (optional)
- cooking spray

Directions:

1. Season chicken with salt and pepper to taste. Place in a shallow dish or plastic bag.
2. Grate orange peel, squeeze orange and reserve 1 tablespoon of juice for the sauce.
3. Pour remaining juice over chicken and marinate for 30 minutes.
4. Mix together the reserved 1 tablespoon of orange juice, barbeque sauce, peanut butter, and 1 teaspoon grated orange peel.
5. Place ¼ cup of sauce mixture in a small bowl for basting. Set remaining sauce aside to serve with cooked chicken.
6. Preheat the toaster oven to 360°F. Spray air fryer oven with nonstick cooking spray.
7. Remove chicken from marinade, letting excess drip off. Place in air fryer oven and air-fry for 5 minutes. Turn chicken over and cook 5 minutes longer.
8. Brush both sides of chicken lightly with sauce.
9. Cook chicken 5 minutes, then turn thighs one more time, again brushing both sides lightly with sauce. Air-fry for 5 more minutes or until chicken is done and juices run clear.
10. Serve chicken with remaining sauce on the side and garnish with chopped peanuts if you like.

Chicken Pot Pie

Servings: 4

Cooking Time: 65 Minutes

Ingredients:

- ¼ cup salted butter
- 1 small sweet onion, chopped
- 1 carrot, chopped

- 1 teaspoon minced garlic
- ¼ cup all-purpose flour
- 1 cup low-sodium chicken broth
- ¼ cup heavy (whipping) cream
- 2 cups diced store-bought rotisserie chicken
- 1 cup frozen peas
- Sea salt, for seasoning
- Freshly ground black pepper, for seasoning
- 1 unbaked store-bought pie crust

Directions:

1. Place the rack in position 1 and preheat the toaster oven to 350°F on BAKE for 5 minutes.
2. Melt the butter in a large saucepan over medium-high heat. Sauté the onion, carrot, and garlic until softened, about 12 minutes. Whisk in the flour to form a thick paste and whisk for 1 minute to cook.
3. Add the broth and whisk until thickened, about 2 minutes. Add the heavy cream, whisking to combine. Add the chicken and peas, and season with salt and pepper.
4. Transfer the filling to a 1½-quart casserole dish and top with the pie crust, tucking the edges into the sides of the casserole dish to completely enclose the filling. Cut 4 or 5 slits in the top of the crust.
5. Bake for 50 minutes until the crust is golden brown and the filling is bubbly. Serve.

Chicken Potpie

Servings: 4

Cooking Time: 48 Minutes

Ingredients:

- Pie filling:
- 1 tablespoon unbleached flour
- ½ cup evaporated skim milk
- 4 skinless, boneless chicken thighs, cut into 1-inch cubes
- 1 cup potatoes, peeled and cut into ½-inch pieces
- ½ cup frozen green peas
- ½ cup thinly sliced carrot
- 2 tablespoons chopped onion
- ½ cup chopped celery
- 1 teaspoon garlic powder
- Salt and freshly ground black pepper to taste
- 8 sheets phyllo pastry, thawed Olive oil

Directions:

1. Preheat the toaster oven to 400° F.
2. Whisk the flour into the milk until smooth in a 1-quart 8½ × 8½ × 4-inch ovenproof baking dish. Add the remaining filling ingredients and mix well. Adjust the seasonings to taste. Cover the dish with aluminum foil.
3. BAKE for 40 minutes, or until the carrot, potatoes, and celery are tender. Remove from the oven and uncover.
4. Place one sheet of phyllo pastry on top of the baked pie-filling mixture, bending the edges to fit the shape of the baking dish. Brush the sheet with olive oil. Add another sheet on top of it and brush with oil. Continue adding the remaining sheets, brushing each one, until the crust is completed. Brush the top with oil.
5. BAKE for 6 minutes, or until the phyllo pastry is browned.

Chicken Souvlaki Gyros

Servings: 4

Cooking Time: 18 Minutes

Ingredients:

- ¼ cup extra-virgin olive oil
- 1 clove garlic, crushed

- 1 tablespoon Italian seasoning
- ½ teaspoon paprika
- ½ lemon, sliced
- ¼ teaspoon salt
- 1 pound boneless, skinless chicken breasts
- 4 whole-grain pita breads
- 1 cup shredded lettuce
- ½ cup chopped tomatoes
- ¼ cup chopped red onion
- ¼ cup cucumber yogurt sauce

Directions:

1. In a large resealable plastic bag, combine the olive oil, garlic, Italian seasoning, paprika, lemon, and salt. Add the chicken to the bag and secure shut. Vigorously shake until all the ingredients are combined. Set in the fridge for 2 hours to marinate.
2. When ready to cook, preheat the toaster oven to 360°F.
3. Liberally spray the air fryer oven with olive oil mist. Remove the chicken from the bag and discard the leftover marinade. Place the chicken into the air fryer oven, allowing enough room between the chicken breasts to flip.
4. Air-fry for 10 minutes, flip, and cook another 8 minutes.
5. Remove the chicken from the air fryer oven when it has cooked (or the internal temperature of the chicken reaches 165°F). Let rest 5 minutes. Then thinly slice the chicken into strips.
6. Assemble the gyros by placing the pita bread on a flat surface and topping with chicken, lettuce, tomatoes, onion, and a drizzle of yogurt sauce.
7. Serve warm.

Chicken Wellington

Servings: 4

Cooking Time: 30 Minutes

Ingredients:

- 2 small (5- to 6-ounce) boneless, skinless chicken breast halves
- Kosher salt and freshly ground black pepper
- 2 teaspoons Italian seasoning
- 2 tablespoons olive oil
- 3 tablespoons unsalted butter, softened
- 3 ounces cream cheese, softened (about ⅓ cup)
- ¾ cup shredded Monterey Jack cheese
- ¼ cup grated Parmesan cheese
- 1 cup frozen (loose-pack) chopped spinach, thawed and squeezed dry
- ¾ cup chopped canned artichoke hearts, drained
- ½ teaspoon garlic powder
- 1 sheet frozen puff pastry, about 9 inches square, thawed (½ of a 17.3-ounce package)
- 1 large egg, lightly beaten

Directions:

1. Preheat the toaster oven to 425° F. Line a 12 x 12-inch baking pan with parchment paper.
2. Cut the chicken breasts in half lengthwise. Season each piece with the salt, pepper, and Italian seasoning. Fold the thinner end under the larger piece to make the chicken breasts into a rounded shape. Secure with toothpicks.
3. Heat a large skillet over medium-high heat. Add the olive oil and heat. Add the chicken breasts and brown well, turning to brown evenly. Remove from the skillet and set aside to cool. Remove the toothpicks.
4. Stir the butter, cream cheese, Monterey Jack, and Parmesan in a large bowl. Stir in the spinach, artichoke hearts, and garlic powder. Season with salt and pepper.

5. Roll out the puff pastry sheet on a lightly floured board until it makes a 12-inch square. Cut into four equal pieces. Spread one-fourth of the spinach-artichoke mixture on the surface of each pastry square to within ½ inch of all four edges. Place the chicken in the center of each. Gently fold the puff pastry up over the chicken and pinch the edges to seal tightly.
6. Place each chicken bundle, seam side down, on the prepared pan. Brush the top of each bundle lightly with the beaten egg. Bake for 25 to 30 minutes, or until the pastry is golden brown and crisp and a meat thermometer inserted into the chicken reaches 165°F.

Jerk Turkey Meatballs

Servings: 7
Cooking Time: 8 Minutes

Ingredients:

- 1 pound lean ground turkey
- ¼ cup chopped onion
- 1 teaspoon minced garlic
- ½ teaspoon dried thyme
- ¼ teaspoon ground cinnamon
- 1 teaspoon cayenne pepper
- ½ teaspoon paprika
- ½ teaspoon salt
- ⅛ teaspoon black pepper
- ¼ teaspoon red pepper flakes
- 2 teaspoons brown sugar
- 1 large egg, whisked
- ⅓ cup panko breadcrumbs
- 2⅓ cups cooked brown Jasmine rice
- 2 green onions, chopped
- ¾ cup sweet onion dressing

Directions:

1. Preheat the toaster oven to 350°F.
2. In a medium bowl, mix the ground turkey with the onion, garlic, thyme, cinnamon, cayenne pepper, paprika, salt, pepper, red pepper flakes, and brown sugar. Add the whisked egg and stir in the breadcrumbs until the turkey starts to hold together.
3. Using a 1-ounce scoop, portion the turkey into meatballs. You should get about 28 meatballs.
4. Spray the air fryer oven with olive oil spray.
5. Place the meatballs into the air fryer oven and air-fry for 5 minutes, rotate the meatball, and cook another 2 to 4 minutes (or until the internal temperature of the meatballs reaches 165°F).
6. Remove the meatballs from the air fryer oven and repeat for the remaining meatballs.
7. Serve warm over a bed of rice with chopped green onions and spicy Caribbean jerk dressing.

Italian Baked Chicken

Servings: 4
Cooking Time: 28 Minutes

Ingredients:

- 1 pound boneless, skinless chicken breasts
- ½ cup dry white wine
- 3 tablespoons olive oil
- 2 tablespoons white wine vinegar
- 2 tablespoons fresh lemon juice
- 2 teaspoons Italian seasoning
- 3 cloves garlic, minced
- ½ teaspoon kosher salt
- ¼ teaspoon freshly ground black pepper
- 4 slices salami, cut in half
- 3 tablespoons shredded Parmesan cheese

Directions:

1. If the chicken breasts are large and thick, slice each breast in half lengthwise. Place the chicken in a shallow baking dish.

2. Combine the white wine, olive oil, vinegar, lemon juice, Italian seasoning, garlic, salt, and pepper in a small bowl. Pour over the chicken breasts. Cover and refrigerate for 2 to 8 hours, turning the chicken occasionally to coat.
3. Preheat the toaster oven to 375 °F.
4. Drain the chicken, discarding the marinade, and place the chicken in an ungreased 12 x 12-inch baking pan. Bake, uncovered, for 20 to 25 minutes or until the chicken is done and a meat thermometer registers 165 °F. Place one slice salami (two pieces) on top of each piece of the chicken. Sprinkle the Parmesan evenly over the chicken breasts and broil for 2 to 3 minutes, or until the cheese is melted and starting to brown.

Fiesta Chicken Plate

Servings: 4
Cooking Time: 15 Minutes

Ingredients:

- 1 pound boneless, skinless chicken breasts (2 large breasts)
- 2 tablespoons lime juice
- 1 teaspoon cumin
- ½ teaspoon salt
- ½ cup grated Pepper Jack cheese
- 1 16-ounce can refried beans
- ½ cup salsa
- 2 cups shredded lettuce
- 1 medium tomato, chopped
- 2 avocados, peeled and sliced
- 1 small onion, sliced into thin rings
- sour cream
- tortilla chips (optional)

Directions:

1. Split each chicken breast in half lengthwise.
2. Mix lime juice, cumin, and salt together and brush on all surfaces of chicken breasts.
3. Place in air fryer oven and air-fry at 390°F for 15 minutes, until well done.
4. Divide the cheese evenly over chicken breasts and air-fry for an additional minute to melt cheese.
5. While chicken is cooking, heat refried beans on stovetop or in microwave.
6. When ready to serve, divide beans among 4 plates. Place chicken breasts on top of beans and spoon salsa over. Arrange the lettuce, tomatoes, and avocados artfully on each plate and scatter with the onion rings.
7. Pass sour cream at the table and serve with tortilla chips if desired.

Turkey-hummus Wraps

Servings: 4
Cooking Time: 7 Minutes

Ingredients:

- 4 large whole wheat wraps
- ½ cup hummus
- 16 thin slices deli turkey
- 8 slices provolone cheese
- 1 cup fresh baby spinach (or more to taste)

Directions:

1. To assemble, place 2 tablespoons of hummus on each wrap and spread to within about a half inch from edges. Top with 4 slices of turkey and 2 slices of provolone. Finish with ¼ cup of baby spinach—or pile on as much as you like.
2. Roll up each wrap. You don't need to fold or seal the ends.
3. Place 2 wraps in air fryer oven, seam side down.

4. Air-fry at 360°F for 4 minutes to warm filling and melt cheese. If you like, you can continue cooking for 3 more minutes, until the wrap is slightly crispy.
5. Repeat step 4 to cook remaining wraps.

Tasty Meat Loaf

Servings: 4
Cooking Time: 35 Minutes

Ingredients:

- 1 to 1½ pounds ground turkey or chicken breast
- 1 egg
- 1 tablespoon chopped fresh parsley
- 2 tablespoons chopped bell pepper
- 3 tablespoons chopped canned mushrooms
- 2 tablespoons chopped onion
- 2 garlic cloves, minced
- ½ cup multigrain bread crumbs
- 1 tablespoon Worcestershire sauce
- 1 tablespoon ketchup
- Freshly ground black pepper to taste

Directions:

1. Preheat the toaster oven to 400° F.
2. Combine all the ingredients in a large bowl and press into a regular-size 4½ × 8½ × 2¼-inch loaf pan.
3. BAKE for 35 minutes, or until browned on top.

Italian Roasted Chicken Thighs

Servings: 6
Cooking Time: 14 Minutes

Ingredients:

- 6 boneless chicken thighs
- ½ teaspoon dried oregano
- ½ teaspoon garlic powder
- ½ teaspoon sea salt
- ½ teaspoon black pepper
- ¼ teaspoon crushed red pepper flakes

Directions:

1. Pat the chicken thighs with paper towel.
2. In a small bowl, mix the oregano, garlic powder, salt, pepper, and crushed red pepper flakes. Rub the spice mixture onto the chicken thighs.
3. Preheat the toaster oven to 400°F.
4. Place the chicken thighs in the air fryer oven and spray with cooking spray. Air-fry for 10 minutes, turn over, and cook another 4 minutes. When cooking completes, the internal temperature should read 165°F.

Crispy Duck With Cherry Sauce

Servings: 2
Cooking Time: 33 Minutes

Ingredients:

- 1 whole duck (up to 5 pounds), split in half, back and rib bones removed
- 1 teaspoon olive oil
- salt and freshly ground black pepper
- Cherry Sauce:
- 1 tablespoon butter
- 1 shallot, minced
- ½ cup sherry
- ¾ cup cherry preserves 1 cup chicken stock
- 1 teaspoon white wine vinegar
- 1 teaspoon fresh thyme leaves
- salt and freshly ground black pepper

Directions:

1. Preheat the toaster oven to 400°F.
2. Trim some of the fat from the duck. Rub olive oil on the duck and season with salt and pepper. Place the duck halves in the air fryer oven,

breast side up and facing the center of the air fryer oven.

3. Air-fry the duck for 20 minutes. Turn the duck over and air-fry for another 6 minutes.

4. While duck is air-frying, make the cherry sauce. Melt the butter in a large sauté pan. Add the shallot and sauté until it is just starting to brown – about 2 to 3 minutes. Add the sherry and deglaze the pan by scraping up any brown bits from the bottom of the pan. Simmer the liquid for a few minutes, until it has reduced by half. Add the cherry preserves, chicken stock and white wine vinegar. Whisk well to combine all the ingredients. Simmer the sauce until it thickens and coats the back of a spoon – about 5 to 7 minutes. Season with salt and pepper and stir in the fresh thyme leaves.

5. When the air fryer oven timer goes off, spoon some cherry sauce over the duck and continue to air-fry at 400°F for 4 more minutes. Then, turn the duck halves back over so that the breast side is facing up. Spoon more cherry sauce over the top of the duck, covering the skin completely. Air-fry for 3 more minutes and then remove the duck to a plate to rest for a few minutes.

6. Serve the duck in halves, or cut each piece in half again for a smaller serving. Spoon any additional sauce over the duck or serve it on the side.

Parmesan Crusted Chicken Cordon Bleu

Servings: 2

Cooking Time: 14 Minutes

Ingredients:

- 2 (6-ounce) boneless, skinless chicken breasts
- salt and freshly ground black pepper
- 1 tablespoon Dijon mustard
- 4 slices Swiss cheese
- 4 slices deli-sliced ham
- ¼ cup all-purpose flour
- 1 egg, beaten
- ¾ cup panko breadcrumbs
- ⅓ cup grated Parmesan cheese
- olive oil, in a spray bottle

Directions:

1. Butterfly the chicken breasts. Place the chicken breast on a cutting board and press down on the breast with the palm of your hand. Slice into the long side of the chicken breast, parallel to the cutting board, but not all the way through to the other side. Open the chicken breast like a "book". Place a piece of plastic wrap over the chicken breast and gently pound it with a meat mallet to make it evenly thick.

2. Season the chicken with salt and pepper. Spread the Dijon mustard on the inside of each chicken breast. Layer one slice of cheese on top of the mustard, then top with the 2 slices of ham and the other slice of cheese.

3. Starting with the long edge of the chicken breast, roll the chicken up to the other side. Secure it shut with 1 or 2 toothpicks.

4. Preheat the toaster oven to 350°F.

5. Set up a dredging station with three shallow dishes. Place the flour in the first dish. Place the beaten egg in the second shallow dish. Combine the panko breadcrumbs and Parmesan cheese together in the third shallow dish. Dip the stuffed and rolled chicken breasts in the flour, then the beaten egg and then roll in the breadcrumb-cheese mixture to cover on all sides. Press the crumbs onto the chicken breasts with your hands to make sure they are well adhered. Spray the

chicken breasts with olive oil and transfer to the air fryer oven.

6. Air-fry at 350°F for 14 minutes, flipping the breasts over halfway through the cooking time. Let the chicken rest for a few minutes before removing the toothpicks, slicing and serving.

Fried Chicken

Servings: 4

Cooking Time: 40 Minutes

Ingredients:

- 12 skin-on chicken drumsticks
- 1 cup buttermilk
- 1½ cups all-purpose flour
- 1 tablespoon smoked paprika
- ¾ teaspoon celery salt
- ¾ teaspoon dried mustard
- ½ teaspoon garlic powder
- ½ teaspoon freshly ground black pepper
- ½ teaspoon sea salt
- ½ teaspoon dried thyme
- ¼ teaspoon dried oregano
- 4 large eggs
- Oil spray (hand-pumped)

Directions:

1. Place the chicken and buttermilk in a medium bowl, cover, and refrigerate for at least 1 hour, up to overnight.
2. Preheat the toaster oven to 375°F on AIR FRY for 5 minutes.
3. In a large bowl, stir the flour, paprika, celery salt, mustard, garlic powder, pepper, salt, thyme, and oregano until well mixed.
4. Beat the eggs until frothy in a medium bowl and set them beside the flour.
5. Place the air-fryer basket in the baking tray and generously spray it with the oil.
6. Dredge a chicken drumstick in the flour, then the eggs, and then in the flour again, thickly coating it, and place the drumstick in the basket. Repeat with 5 more drumsticks and spray them all lightly with the oil on all sides.
7. In position 2, air fry for 20 minutes, turning halfway through, until golden brown and crispy with an internal temperature of 165°F.
8. Repeat with the remaining chicken, covering the cooked chicken loosely with foil to keep it warm. Serve.

Chicken Nuggets

Servings: 20

Cooking Time: 14 Minutes

Ingredients:

- 1 pound boneless, skinless chicken thighs, cut into 1-inch chunks
- ¾ teaspoon salt
- ½ teaspoon black pepper
- ½ teaspoon garlic powder
- ½ teaspoon onion powder
- ½ cup flour
- 2 eggs, beaten
- ½ cup panko breadcrumbs
- 3 tablespoons plain breadcrumbs
- oil for misting or cooking spray

Directions:

1. In the bowl of a food processor, combine chicken, ½ teaspoon salt, pepper, garlic powder, and onion powder. Process in short pulses until chicken is very finely chopped and well blended.
2. Place flour in one shallow dish and beaten eggs in another. In a third dish or plastic bag, mix together the panko crumbs, plain breadcrumbs, and ¼ teaspoon salt.

3. Shape chicken mixture into small nuggets. Dip nuggets in flour, then eggs, then panko crumb mixture.
4. Spray nuggets on both sides with oil or cooking spray and place in air fryer oven in a single layer, close but not overlapping.
5. Air-fry at 360°F for 10 minutes. Spray with oil and cook 4 minutes, until chicken is done and coating is golden brown.
6. Repeat step 5 to cook remaining nuggets.

Marinated Green Pepper And Pineapple Chicken

Servings: 4
Cooking Time: 20 Minutes

Ingredients:

- Marinade:
- 1 teaspoon finely chopped fresh ginger
- 2 garlic cloves, finely chopped
- 1 teaspoon toasted sesame oil
- 1 tablespoon brown sugar
- 2 tablespoons soy sauce
- ¾ cup dry white wine
- 2 skinless, boneless chicken breasts, cut into 1 × 3-inch strips
- 2 tablespoons chopped onion
- 1 bell pepper, chopped
- 1 5-ounce can pineapple chunks, drained
- 2 tablespoons grated unsweetened coconut

Directions:

1. Combine the marinade ingredients in a medium bowl and blend well. Add the chicken strips and spoon the mixture over them. Marinate in the refrigerator for at least 1 hour. Remove the strips from the marinade and place in an oiled or nonstick 8½ × 8½ × 2-inch square (cake) pan. Add the onion and pepper and mix well.
2. BROIL for 8 minutes. Then remove from the oven and, using tongs, turn the chicken, pepper, and onion pieces. (Spoon the reserved marinade over the pieces, if desired.)
3. BROIL again for 8 minutes, or until the chicken, pepper, and onion are cooked through and tender. Add the pineapple chunks and coconut and toss to mix well.
4. BROIL for another 4 minutes, or until the coconut is lightly browned.

VEGETABLES AND VEGETARIAN

Fried Cauliflowerwith Parmesan Lemon Dressing

Servings: 2

Cooking Time: 12 Minutes

Ingredients:

- 4 cups cauliflower florets (about half a large head)
- 1 tablespoon olive oil
- salt and freshly ground black pepper
- 1 teaspoon finely chopped lemon zest
- 1 tablespoon fresh lemon juice (about half a lemon)
- ¼ cup grated Parmigiano-Reggiano cheese
- 4 tablespoons extra virgin olive oil
- ¼ teaspoon salt
- lots of freshly ground black pepper
- 1 tablespoon chopped fresh parsley

Directions:

1. Preheat the toaster oven to 400°F.
2. Toss the cauliflower florets with the olive oil, salt and freshly ground black pepper. Air-fry for 12 minutes.
3. While the cauliflower is frying, make the dressing. Combine the lemon zest, lemon juice, Parmigiano-Reggiano cheese and olive oil in a small bowl. Season with salt and lots of freshly ground black pepper. Stir in the parsley.
4. Turn the fried cauliflower out onto a serving platter and drizzle the dressing over the top.

Brown Rice And Goat Cheese Croquettes

Servings: 3

Cooking Time: 8 Minutes

Ingredients:

- ¾ cup Water
- 6 tablespoons Raw medium-grain brown rice, such as brown Arborio
- ½ cup Shredded carrot
- ¼ cup Walnut pieces
- 3 tablespoons (about 1½ ounces) Soft goat cheese
- 1 tablespoon Pasteurized egg substitute, such as Egg Beaters (gluten-free, if a concern)
- ¼ teaspoon Dried thyme
- ¼ teaspoon Table salt
- ¼ teaspoon Ground black pepper
- Olive oil spray

Directions:

1. Combine the water, rice, and carrots in a small saucepan set over medium-high heat. Bring to a boil, stirring occasionally. Cover, reduce the heat to very low, and simmer very slowly for 45 minutes, or until the water has been absorbed and the rice is tender. Set aside, covered, for 10 minutes.
2. Scrape the contents of the saucepan into a food processor. Cool for 10 minutes.
3. Preheat the toaster oven to 400°F.
4. Put the nuts, cheese, egg substitute, thyme, salt, and pepper into the food processor. Cover and pulse to a coarse paste, stopping the machine at least once to scrape down the inside of the canister.
5. Uncover the food processor; scrape down and remove the blade. Using wet, clean hands, form the mixture into two 4-inch-diameter patties for a small batch, three 4-inch-diameter patties for a

medium batch, or four 4-inch-diameter patties for a large one. Generously coat both sides of the patties with olive oil spray.

6. Set the patties in the air fryer oven with as much air space between them as possible. Air-fry undisturbed for 8 minutes, or until brown and crisp.

7. Use a nonstick-safe spatula to transfer the croquettes to a wire rack. Cool for 5 minutes before serving.

Latkes

Servings: 12

Cooking Time: 13 Minutes

Ingredients:

- 1 russet potato
- ¼ onion
- 2 eggs, lightly beaten
- ⅓ cup flour
- ½ teaspoon baking powder
- 1 teaspoon salt
- freshly ground black pepper
- canola or vegetable oil, in a spray bottle
- chopped chives, for garnish
- apple sauce
- sour cream

Directions:

1. Shred the potato and onion with a coarse box grater or a food processor with the shredding blade. Place the shredded vegetables into a colander or mesh strainer and squeeze or press down firmly to remove the excess water.
2. Transfer the onion and potato to a large bowl and add the eggs, flour, baking powder, salt and black pepper. Mix to combine and then shape the mixture into patties, about ¼-cup of mixture each. Brush or spray both sides of the latkes with oil.
3. Preheat the toaster oven to 400°F.
4. Air-fry the latkes in batches. Transfer one layer of the latkes to the air fryer oven and air-fry at 400°F for 12 to 13 minutes, flipping them over halfway through the cooking time. Transfer the finished latkes to a platter and cover with aluminum foil, or place them in a warm oven to keep warm.
5. Garnish the latkes with chopped chives and serve with sour cream and applesauce.

Pimiento-and-olive Stuffed Potatoes

Servings: 2

Cooking Time: 8 Minutes

Ingredients:

- 2 large baking potatoes, baked
- Stuffing:
- 3 tablespoons minced pimientos
- 3 tablespoons pitted and chopped black olives
- 3 tablespoons nonfat sour cream
- 1 teaspoon paprika
- Salt and butcher's pepper to taste

Directions:

1. Scoop out the pulp of the baked potatoes and place in a bowl.
2. Add the stuffing ingredients, blending well, and fill the potato shells. Place the potatoes on a broiling rack with a pan underneath.
3. BROIL for 8 minutes, or until the top is lightly browned.

Wilted Brussels Sprout Slaw

Servings: 4

Cooking Time: 18 Minutes

Ingredients:

- 2 Thick-cut bacon strip(s), halved widthwise (gluten-free, if a concern)
- 4½ cups (about 1 pound 2 ounces) Bagged shredded Brussels sprouts
- ¼ teaspoon Table salt
- 2 tablespoons White balsamic vinegar
- 2 teaspoons Worcestershire sauce (gluten-free, if a concern)
- 1 teaspoon Dijon mustard (gluten-free, if a concern)
- ¼ teaspoon Ground black pepper

Directions:

1. Preheat the toaster oven to 375°F .
2. When the machine is at temperature, lay the bacon strip halves in the air fryer oven in one layer and air-fry for 10 minutes, or until crisp.
3. Use kitchen tongs to transfer the bacon pieces to a wire rack. Put the shredded Brussels sprouts in a large bowl. Drain any fat from the pan or the tray under the pan onto the Brussels sprouts. Add the salt and toss well to coat.
4. Put the Brussels sprout shreds in the air fryer oven, spreading them out into as close to an even layer as you can. Air-fry for 8 minutes, tossing the air fryer oven's contents at least three times, until wilted and lightly browned.
5. Pour the contents of the air fryer oven into a serving bowl. Chop the bacon and add it to the Brussels sprouts. Add the vinegar, Worcestershire sauce, mustard, and pepper. Toss well to blend the dressing and coat the Brussels sprout shreds. Serve warm.

Yellow Squash With Bell Peppers

Servings: 4

Cooking Time: 50 Minutes

Ingredients:

- Squash mixture:
- 2 cups yellow (summer) squash, thinly sliced
- ⅓ cup dry white wine
- 1 bell pepper, seeded and sliced into thin strips
- 1 6½-ounce jar marinated artichoke hearts, drained and sliced
- 1 tablespoon minced fresh garlic
- 1 5-ounce can diced pimientos, drained
- Salt and freshly ground black pepper to taste
- ¼ cup shredded part-skim mozzarella cheese
- 3 tablespoons Homemade Bread Crumbs
- 2 tablespoons chopped fresh cilantro

Directions:

1. Preheat the toaster oven to 400° F.
2. Combine the squash mixture ingredients in a 1-quart 8½ × 8½ × 4-inch ovenproof baking dish, mixing well. Adjust the seasonings.
3. BAKE, covered, for 40 minutes, or until the vegetables are tender. Uncover and sprinkle with the cheese and bread crumbs.
4. BROIL 10 minutes, or until the top is lightly browned. Garnish with the chopped cilantro before serving.

Salmon Salad With Steamboat Dressing

Servings: 4

Cooking Time: 18 Minutes

Ingredients:

- ¼ teaspoon salt
- 1½ teaspoons dried dill weed

- 1 tablespoon fresh lemon juice
- 8 ounces fresh or frozen salmon fillet (skin on)
- 8 cups shredded romaine, Boston, or other leaf lettuce
- 8 spears cooked asparagus, cut in 1-inch pieces
- 8 cherry tomatoes, halved or quartered

Directions:

1. Mix the salt and dill weed together. Rub the lemon juice over the salmon on both sides and sprinkle the dill and salt all over. Refrigerate for 15 to 20 minutes.
2. Make Steamboat Dressing and refrigerate while cooking salmon and preparing salad.
3. Cook salmon in air fryer oven at 330°F for 18 minutes. Cooking time will vary depending on thickness of fillets. When done, salmon should flake with fork but still be moist and tender.
4. Remove salmon from air fryer oven and cool slightly. At this point, the skin should slide off easily. Cut salmon into 4 pieces and discard skin.
5. Divide the lettuce among 4 plates. Scatter asparagus spears and tomato pieces evenly over the lettuce, allowing roughly 2 whole spears and 2 whole cherry tomatoes per plate.
6. Top each salad with one portion of the salmon and drizzle with a tablespoon of dressing. Serve with additional dressing to pass at the table.

Panzanella Salad With Crispy Croutons

Servings: 4

Cooking Time: 3 Minutes

Ingredients:

- ½ French baguette, sliced in half lengthwise
- 2 large cloves garlic
- 2 large ripe tomatoes, divided
- 2 small Persian cucumbers, quartered and diced
- ¼ cup Kalamata olives
- 1 tablespoon chopped, fresh oregano or 1 teaspoon dried oregano
- ¼ cup chopped fresh basil
- ¼ cup chopped fresh parsley
- ½ cup sliced red onion
- 2 tablespoons red wine vinegar
- ¼ cup extra-virgin olive oil
- Salt and pepper, to taste

Directions:

1. Preheat the toaster oven to 380°F.
2. Place the baguette into the air fryer oven and toast for 3 to 5 minutes or until lightly golden brown.
3. Remove the bread from air fryer oven and immediately rub 1 raw garlic clove firmly onto the inside portion of each piece of bread, scraping the garlic onto the bread.
4. Slice 1 of the tomatoes in half and rub the cut edge of one half of the tomato onto the toasted bread. Season the rubbed bread with sea salt to taste.
5. Cut the bread into cubes and place in a large bowl. Cube the remaining 1½ tomatoes and add to the bowl. Add the cucumbers, olives, oregano, basil, parsley, and onion; stir to mix. Drizzle the red wine vinegar into the bowl, and stir. Drizzle the olive oil over the top, stir, and adjust the seasonings with salt and pepper.
6. Serve immediately or allow to sit at room temperature up to 1 hour before serving.

Fingerling Potatoes

Servings: 4

Cooking Time: 15 Minutes

Ingredients:

- 1 pound fingerling potatoes
- 1 tablespoon light olive oil
- ½ teaspoon dried parsley
- ½ teaspoon lemon juice
- coarsely ground sea salt

Directions:

1. Cut potatoes in half lengthwise.
2. In a large bowl, combine potatoes, oil, parsley, and lemon juice. Stir well to coat potatoes.
3. Place potatoes in air fryer oven and air-fry at 360°F for 15 minutes or until lightly browned and tender inside.
4. Sprinkle with sea salt before serving.

Zucchini Boats With Ham And Cheese

Servings: 4

Cooking Time: 12 Minutes

Ingredients:

- 2 6-inch-long zucchini
- 2 ounces Thinly sliced deli ham, any rind removed, meat roughly chopped
- 4 Dry-packed sun-dried tomatoes, chopped
- ⅓ cup Purchased pesto
- ¼ cup Packaged mini croutons
- ¼ cup (about 1 ounce) Shredded semi-firm mozzarella cheese

Directions:

1. Preheat the toaster oven to 375°F .
2. Split the zucchini in half lengthwise and use a flatware spoon or a serrated grapefruit spoon to scoop out the insides of the halves, leaving at least a ¼-inch border all around the zucchini half. (You can save the scooped out insides to add to soups and stews—or even freeze it for a much later use.)
3. Mix the ham, sun-dried tomatoes, pesto, croutons, and half the cheese in a bowl until well combined. Pack this mixture into the zucchini "shells." Top them with the remaining cheese.
4. Set them stuffing side up in the air fryer oven without touching (even a fraction of an inch between them is enough room). Air-fry undisturbed for 12 minutes, or until softened and browned, with the cheese melted on top.
5. Use a nonstick-safe spatula to transfer the zucchini boats stuffing side up on a wire rack. Cool for 5 or 10 minutes before serving.

Homemade Potato Puffs

Servings: 4

Cooking Time: 15 Minutes

Ingredients:

- 1¾ cups Water
- 4 tablespoons (¼ cup/½ stick) Butter
- 2 cups plus 2 tablespoons Instant mashed potato flakes
- 1½ teaspoons Table salt
- ¾ teaspoon Ground black pepper
- ¼ teaspoon Mild paprika
- ¼ teaspoon Dried thyme
- 1¼ cups Seasoned Italian-style dried bread crumbs (gluten-free, if a concern)
- Olive oil spray

Directions:

1. Heat the water with the butter in a medium saucepan set over medium-low heat just until the butter melts. Do not bring to a boil.

2. Remove the saucepan from the heat and stir in the potato flakes, salt, pepper, paprika, and thyme until smooth. Set aside to cool for 5 minutes.
3. Preheat the toaster oven to 400°F. Spread the bread crumbs on a dinner plate.
4. Scrape up 2 tablespoons of the potato flake mixture and form it into a small, oblong puff, like a little cylinder about 1½ inches long. Gently roll the puff in the bread crumbs until coated on all sides. Set it aside and continue making more, about 12 for the small batch, 18 for the medium batch, or 24 for the large.
5. Coat the potato cylinders with olive oil spray on all sides, then arrange them in the air fryer oven in one layer with some air space between them. Air-fry undisturbed for 15 minutes, or until crisp and brown.
6. Gently dump the contents of the air fryer oven onto a wire rack. Cool for 5 minutes before serving.

Crispy Noodle Salad

Servings: 3
Cooking Time: 22 Minutes

Ingredients:

- 6 ounces Fresh Chinese-style stir-fry or lo mein wheat noodles
- 1½ tablespoons Cornstarch
- ¾ cup Chopped stemmed and cored red bell pepper
- 2 Medium scallion(s), trimmed and thinly sliced
- 2 teaspoons Sambal oelek or other pulpy hot red pepper sauce
- 2 teaspoons Thai sweet chili sauce or red ketchup-like chili sauce, such as Heinz
- 2 teaspoons Regular or low-sodium soy sauce or tamari sauce
- 2 teaspoons Unseasoned rice vinegar
- 1 tablespoon White or black sesame seeds

Directions:

1. Bring a large saucepan of water to a boil over high heat. Add the noodles and boil for 2 minutes. Drain in a colander set in the sink. Rinse several times with cold water, shaking the colander to drain the noodles very well. Spread the noodles out on a large cutting board and air-dry for 10 minutes.
2. Preheat the toaster oven to 400°F.
3. Toss the noodles in a bowl with the cornstarch until well coated. Spread them out across the entire air fryer oven (although they will be touching and overlapping a bit). Air-fry for 6 minutes, then turn the solid mass of noodles over as one piece. If it cracks in half or smaller pieces, just fit these back together after turning. Continue air-frying for 6 minutes, or until golden brown and crisp.
4. As the noodles cook, stir the bell pepper, scallion(s), sambal oelek, red chili sauce, soy sauce, vinegar, and sesame seeds in a serving bowl until well combined.
5. Turn the air fryer oven of noodles out onto a cutting board and cool for a minute or two. Break the mass of noodles into individual noodles and/or small chunks and add to the dressing in the serving bowl. Toss well to serve.

Fried Corn On The Cob

Servings: 2

Cooking Time: 10 Minutes

Ingredients:

- 1½ tablespoons Regular or low-fat mayonnaise (not fat-free; gluten-free, if a concern)
- 1½ teaspoons Minced garlic
- ¼ teaspoon Table salt
- ¾ cup Plain panko bread crumbs (gluten-free, if a concern)
- 3 4-inch lengths husked and de-silked corn on the cob
- Vegetable oil spray

Directions:

1. Preheat the toaster oven to 400°F.
2. Stir the mayonnaise, garlic, and salt in a small bowl until well combined. Spread the panko on a dinner plate.
3. Brush the mayonnaise mixture over the kernels of a piece of corn on the cob. Set the corn in the bread crumbs, then roll, pressing gently, to coat it. Lightly coat with vegetable oil spray. Set it aside, then coat the remaining piece(s) of corn in the same way.
4. Set the coated corn on the cob in the air fryer oven with as much air space between the pieces as possible. Air-fry undisturbed for 10 minutes, or until brown and crisp along the coating.
5. Use kitchen tongs to gently transfer the pieces of corn to a wire rack. Cool for 5 minutes before serving.

Roasted Belgian Endive With Pistachios And Lemon

Servings: 2

Cooking Time: 7 Minutes

Ingredients:

- 2 Medium 3-ounce Belgian endive head(s)
- 2 tablespoons Olive oil
- ½ teaspoon Table salt
- ¼ cup Finely chopped unsalted shelled pistachios
- Up to 2 teaspoons Lemon juice

Directions:

1. Preheat the toaster oven to 325°F (or 330°F, if that's the closest setting).
2. Trim the Belgian endive head(s), removing the little bit of dried-out stem end but keeping the leaves intact. Quarter the head(s) through the stem (which will hold the leaves intact). Brush the endive quarters with oil, getting it down between the leaves. Sprinkle the quarters with salt.
3. When the machine is at temperature, set the endive quarters cut sides up in the air fryer oven with as much air space between them as possible. They should not touch. Air-fry undisturbed for 7 minutes, or until lightly browned along the edges.
4. Use kitchen tongs to transfer the endive quarters to serving plates or a platter. Sprinkle with the pistachios and lemon juice. Serve warm or at room temperature.

Grits Casserole

Servings: 4

Cooking Time: 30 Minutes

Ingredients:

- 10 fresh asparagus spears, cut into 1-inch pieces
- 2 cups cooked grits, cooled to room temperature
- 1 egg, beaten
- 2 teaspoons Worcestershire sauce
- ½ teaspoon garlic powder

- ¼ teaspoon salt
- 2 slices provolone cheese (about 1½ ounces)
- oil for misting or cooking spray

Directions:

1. Mist asparagus spears with oil and air-fry at 390°F for 5 minutes, until crisp-tender.
2. In a medium bowl, mix together the grits, egg, Worcestershire, garlic powder, and salt.
3. Spoon half of grits mixture into air fryer oven baking pan and top with asparagus.
4. Tear cheese slices into pieces and layer evenly on top of asparagus.
5. Top with remaining grits.
6. Bake at 360°F for 25 minutes. The casserole will rise a little as it cooks. When done, the top will have browned lightly with just a hint of crispiness.

Eggplant And Tomato Slices

Servings: 4

Cooking Time: 36 Minutes

Ingredients:

- 2 tablespoons olive oil
- ¼ teaspoon garlic powder
- 4½-inch-thick slices eggplant
- 4 ¼-inch-thick slices fresh tomato
- 2 tablespoons tomato sauce or salsa
- ½ cup shredded Parmesan cheese
- Salt and freshly ground black pepper to taste
- 2 tablespoons chopped fresh basil, cilantro, parsley, or oregano

Directions:

1. Whisk together the oil and garlic powder in a small bowl. Brush each eggplant slice with the mixture and place in an oiled or nonstick 8½ × 8½ × 2-inch square baking (cake) pan.
2. BROIL for 20 minutes. Remove the pan from the oven and turn the pieces with tongs. Top each with a slice of tomato and broil another 10 minutes, or until tender. Remove the pan from the oven, brush each slice with tomato sauce or salsa, and sprinkle generously with Parmesan cheese. Season to taste with salt and pepper. Broil again for 6 minutes, until the tops are browned.
3. Garnish with the fresh herb and serve.

Five-spice Roasted Sweet Potatoes

Servings: 4

Cooking Time: 12 Minutes

Ingredients:

- ½ teaspoon ground cinnamon
- ¼ teaspoon ground cumin
- ¼ teaspoon paprika
- 1 teaspoon chile powder
- ⅛ teaspoon turmeric
- ½ teaspoon salt (optional)
- freshly ground black pepper
- 2 large sweet potatoes, peeled and cut into ¾-inch cubes (about 3 cups)
- 1 tablespoon olive oil

Directions:

1. In a large bowl, mix together cinnamon, cumin, paprika, chile powder, turmeric, salt, and pepper to taste.
2. Add potatoes and stir well.
3. Drizzle the seasoned potatoes with the olive oil and stir until evenly coated.
4. Place seasoned potatoes in the air fryer oven baking pan or an ovenproof dish that fits inside your air fryer oven.
5. Air-fry for 6 minutes at 390°F, stop, and stir well.
6. Air-fry for an additional 6 minutes.

Crunchy Roasted Potatoes

Servings: 5

Cooking Time: 25 Minutes

Ingredients:

- 2 pounds Small (1- to 1½-inch-diameter) red, white, or purple potatoes
- 2 tablespoons Olive oil
- 2 teaspoons Table salt
- ¾ teaspoon Garlic powder
- ½ teaspoon Ground black pepper

Directions:

1. Preheat the toaster oven to 400°F.
2. Toss the potatoes, oil, salt, garlic powder, and pepper in a large bowl until the spuds are evenly and thoroughly coated.
3. When the machine is at temperature, pour the potatoes into the air fryer oven, spreading them into an even layer (although they may be stacked on top of each other). Air-fry for 25 minutes, tossing twice, until the potatoes are tender but crunchy.
4. Pour the contents of the air fryer oven into a serving bowl. Cool for 5 minutes before serving.

Rolled Chinese (napa) Cabbage With Chickpea Filling

Servings: 4

Cooking Time: 46 Minutes

Ingredients:

- 6 Chinese cabbage leaves, approximately 7 inches long
- Filling:
- 2 tablespoons low-fat ricotta cheese or Yogurt Cheese Spread
- 1 cup canned chickpeas (garbanzos), drained and mashed
- 1 teaspoon lemon juice
- Salt and butcher's pepper to taste
- 2 tablespoons olive oil for brushing
- 2 tablespoons chopped almonds

Directions:

1. Layer an 8½ × 8½ × 2-inch square baking (cake) pan with the cabbage leaves and add enough water to barely cover them.
2. BROIL 5 minutes, turn the leaves with tongs, and broil another 5 minutes, or until the leaves are partially cooked and just pliable. Spread the leaves on paper towels to drain and cool.
3. Mix the filling ingredients together in a medium bowl and adjust the seasonings to taste. Place equal portions of filling 2 inches from the stem end (base of the leaf) and roll up the leaf, enclosing the filling. Place each roll with the leaf edge down in an oiled or 8½ × 8½ × 2-inch square baking (cake) pan. Sprinkle with the almonds. Cover the pan with aluminum foil.
4. BAKE at 400° F. for 30 minutes, or until the rolls are tender. Remove the cover.
5. BROIL 6 minutes, or until the almonds and cabbage leaves are lightly browned.

Fried Green Tomatoes With Sriracha Mayo

Servings: 4

Cooking Time: 12 Minutes

Ingredients:

- 3 green tomatoes
- salt and freshly ground black pepper
- ⅓ cup all-purpose flour
- 2 eggs
- ½ cup buttermilk
- 1 cup panko breadcrumbs
- 1 cup cornmeal

- olive oil, in a spray bottle
- fresh thyme sprigs or chopped fresh chives
- Sriracha Mayo
- ½ cup mayonnaise
- 1 to 2 tablespoons sriracha hot sauce
- 1 tablespoon milk

Directions:

1. Cut the tomatoes in ¼-inch slices. Pat them dry with a clean kitchen towel and season generously with salt and pepper.
2. Set up a dredging station using three shallow dishes. Place the flour in the first shallow dish, whisk the eggs and buttermilk together in the second dish, and combine the panko breadcrumbs and cornmeal in the third dish.
3. Preheat the toaster oven to 400°F.
4. Dredge the tomato slices in flour to coat on all sides. Then dip them into the egg mixture and finally press them into the breadcrumbs to coat all sides of the tomato.
5. Spray or brush the air-fryer oven with olive oil. Transfer 3 to 4 tomato slices into the air fryer oven and spray the top with olive oil. Air-fry the tomatoes at 400°F for 8 minutes. Flip them over, spray the other side with oil and air-fry for an additional 4 minutes until golden brown.
6. While the tomatoes are cooking, make the sriracha mayo. Combine the mayonnaise, 1 tablespoon of the sriracha hot sauce and milk in a small bowl. Stir well until the mixture is smooth. Add more sriracha sauce to taste.
7. When the tomatoes are done, transfer them to a cooling rack or a platter lined with paper towels so the bottom does not get soggy. Before serving, carefully stack the all the tomatoes into air fryer oven and air-fry at 350°F for 1 to 2 minutes to heat them back up.
8. Serve the fried green tomatoes hot with the sriracha mayo on the side. Season one last time with salt and freshly ground black pepper and garnish with sprigs of fresh thyme or chopped fresh chives.

Roasted Corn Salad

Servings: 3

Cooking Time: 15 Minutes

Ingredients:

- 3 4-inch lengths husked and de-silked corn on the cob
- Olive oil spray
- 1 cup Packed baby arugula leaves
- 12 Cherry tomatoes, halved
- Up to 3 Medium scallion(s), trimmed and thinly sliced
- 2 tablespoons Lemon juice
- 1 tablespoon Olive oil
- 1½ teaspoons Honey
- ¼ teaspoon Mild paprika
- ¼ teaspoon Dried oregano
- ¼ teaspoon, plus more to taste Table salt
- ¼ teaspoon Ground black pepper

Directions:

1. Preheat the toaster oven to 400°F.
2. When the machine is at temperature, lightly coat the pieces of corn on the cob with olive oil spray. Set the pieces of corn in the air fryer oven with as much air space between them as possible. Air-fry undisturbed for 15 minutes, or until the corn is charred in a few spots.
3. Use kitchen tongs to transfer the corn to a wire rack. Cool for 15 minutes.
4. Cut the kernels off the ears by cutting the fat end off each piece so it will stand up straight on a cutting board, then running a knife down the

corn. (Or you can save your fingers and buy a fancy tool to remove kernels from corn cobs. Check it out at online kitchenware stores.) Scoop the kernels into a serving bowl.

5. Chop the arugula into bite-size bits and add these to the kernels. Add the tomatoes and scallions, too. Whisk the lemon juice, olive oil, honey, paprika, oregano, salt, and pepper in a small bowl until the honey dissolves. Pour over the salad and toss well to coat, tasting for extra salt before serving.

Roasted Root Vegetables With Cinnamon

Servings: 4

Cooking Time: 20 Minutes

Ingredients:

- 1 small sweet potato, cut into 1-inch pieces
- 2 carrots, cut into 1-inch pieces
- 2 parsnips, cut into 1-inch pieces
- 2 tablespoons brown sugar (dark or light)
- 1 tablespoon olive oil
- ¼ teaspoon ground cinnamon
- Oil spray (hand-pumped)
- Sea salt, for seasoning

Directions:

1. Preheat the toaster oven to 350°F on AIR FRY for 5 minutes.
2. In a large bowl, toss the sweet potato, carrots, parsnips, brown sugar, oil, and cinnamon until well mixed.
3. Place the air-fryer basket in the baking tray and generously spray the mesh with oil.
4. Spread the vegetables in the basket and air fry in position 2 for 20 minutes, shaking the basket after 10 minutes, until the vegetables are tender and lightly caramelized.
5. Season with salt and serve.

Sweet Potato Curly Fries

Servings: 4

Cooking Time: 10 Minutes

Ingredients:

- 2 medium sweet potatoes, washed
- 2 tablespoons avocado oil
- ¾ teaspoon salt, divided
- 1 medium avocado
- ½ teaspoon garlic powder
- ½ teaspoon paprika
- ¼ teaspoon black pepper
- ½ juice lime
- 3 tablespoons fresh cilantro

Directions:

1. Preheat the toaster oven to 400°F.
2. Using a spiralizer, create curly spirals with the sweet potatoes. Keep the pieces about 1½ inches long. Continue until all the potatoes are used.
3. In a large bowl, toss the curly sweet potatoes with the avocado oil and ½ teaspoon of the salt.
4. Place the potatoes in the air fryer oven and air-fry for 5 minutes; cook another 5 minutes.
5. While cooking, add the avocado, garlic, paprika, pepper, the remaining ¼ teaspoon of salt, lime juice, and cilantro to a blender and process until smooth. Set aside.
6. When cooking completes, remove the fries and serve warm with the lime avocado sauce.

Baked Stuffed Acorn Squash

Servings: 2

Cooking Time: 25 Minutes

Ingredients:

- Stuffing:
- ¼ cup multigrain bread crumbs

- 1 tablespoon olive oil
- ¼ cup canned or frozen thawed corn
- 2 tablespoons chopped onion
- 1 teaspoon capers
- 1 teaspoon garlic powder
- Salt and freshly ground black pepper
- 1 medium acorn squash, halved and seeds scooped out

Directions:

1. Preheat the toaster oven to 400° F.
2. Combine the stuffing ingredients and season to taste. Fill the squash cavities with the mixture and place in an oiled or nonstick 8½ × 8½ × 2-inch square baking (cake) pan.
3. BAKE for 25 minutes, or until the squash is tender and the stuffing is lightly browned.

Honey-roasted Parsnips

Servings: 3

Cooking Time: 23 Minutes

Ingredients:

- 1½ pounds Medium parsnips, peeled
- Olive oil spray
- 1 tablespoon Honey
- 1½ teaspoons Water
- ¼ teaspoon Table salt

Directions:

1. Preheat the toaster oven to 350°F .
2. If the thick end of a parsnip is more than ½ inch in diameter, cut the parsnip just below where it swells to its large end, then slice the large section in half lengthwise. Generously coat the parsnips on all sides with olive oil spray.
3. When the machine is at temperature, set the parsnips in the air fryer oven with as much air space between them as possible. Air-fry undisturbed for 20 minutes.
4. Whisk the honey, water, and salt in a small bowl until smooth. Brush this mixture over the parsnips. Air-fry undisturbed for 3 minutes more, or until the glaze is lightly browned.
5. Use kitchen tongs to transfer the parsnips to a wire rack or a serving platter. Cool for a couple of minutes before serving.

Broccoli With Chinese Mushrooms And Water Chestnuts

Servings: 4

Cooking Time: 20 Minutes

Ingredients:

- 2 cups broccoli florets, cut in half
- ½ cup Chinese dried mushrooms, cooked, drained, stemmed, and sliced
- ¼ cup dry white wine
- 1 5-ounce can sliced water chestnuts, well drained
- 1 tablespoon vegetable oil
- 1 teaspoon toasted sesame oil
- 1 teaspoon oyster sauce

Directions:

1. Combine all the ingredients with ¼ cup water in an oiled or nonstick 8½ × 8½ × 2-inch square baking (cake) pan. Adjust the seasonings to taste.
2. BROIL 20 minutes, turning with tongs every 5 minutes, or until the vegetables are tender.

Lentil-stuffed Zucchini

Servings: 2

Cooking Time: 50 Minutes

Ingredients:

- 2 large zucchini
- 2 teaspoons olive oil

- 1 (15-ounce) can low-sodium lentils, drained and rinsed
- 1 large tomato, chopped
- 1 scallion, both white and green parts, chopped
- ½ jalapeño pepper, minced
- ½ cup corn kernels, fresh or frozen (thawed)
- 1 tablespoon fresh cilantro, chopped
- 1 teaspoon minced garlic
- 1 teaspoon ground cumin
- ¼ teaspoon chili powder
- ½ cup shredded Monterey Jack cheese

Directions:

1. Preheat the toaster oven to 400°F on BAKE for 5 minutes.
2. Line the baking tray with parchment paper.
3. Cut the zucchini in half lengthwise and scoop out the insides so that you have a hollow shell (about ¼-inch thick all the way around).
4. Lightly oil both sides of the zucchini shells and set them on the baking sheet.
5. In a large bowl, stir the lentils, tomato, scallion, jalapeño, corn, cilantro, garlic, cumin, and chili powder until well mixed.
6. Spoon the lentil mixture into the zucchini and top with the cheese.
7. Bake for 50 minutes. The zucchini should be tender, the filling heated through, and the cheese melted and lightly browned. Serve.

Potatoes Au Gratin

Servings: 4

Cooking Time: 40 Minutes

Ingredients:

- Mixture:
- ½ cup fat-free half-and-half
- ¼ cup nonfat plain yogurt
- 2 tablespoons margarine
- 2 tablespoons unbleached flour
- 1 teaspoon garlic powder
- ¼ cup shredded low-fat mozzarella cheese
- 2 tablespoons grated Parmesan cheese
- Salt and butcher's pepper to taste
- 2 cups peeled and diced potatoes
- ½ cup chopped onion
- 1 tablespoon fresh or frozen chives
- ¼ teaspoon paprika

Directions:

1. Preheat the toaster oven to 400° F.
2. Process the mixture ingredients in a food processor or blender until smooth. Pour into a 1-quart 8½ × 8½ × 4-inch ovenproof baking dish.
3. Add the potatoes, onion, chives, and paprika and stir to mix well. Cover the dish with aluminum foil.
4. BAKE, covered, for 40 minutes, or until the potatoes and onion are tender.

DESSERTS

Sour Cream Pound Cake

Servings: 6

Cooking Time: 60 Minutes

Ingredients:

- ¾ cup unsalted butter, plus extra for greasing the baking pan
- 2½ cups all-purpose flour, sifted, plus extra for dusting the baking pan
- 1½ cups granulated sugar
- 4 large eggs
- 2 teaspoons pure vanilla extract
- ½ teaspoon baking soda
- ¾ cup sour cream

Directions:

1. Place the rack in position 1 and preheat the toaster oven to 350°F on BAKE for 5 minutes.
2. Lightly grease and dust a 9-by-5-inch loaf pan.
3. In a large bowl, cream the butter and sugar with an electric hand beater until very light and fluffy, about 4 minutes.
4. Beat in the eggs one at a time, scraping down the sides of the bowl after each addition.
5. Beat in the vanilla.
6. In a medium bowl, stir the flour and baking soda.
7. Fold the flour mixture and sour cream into the butter mixture, alternating two times each, until well combined.
8. Spoon the batter into the loaf pan and bake for 1 hour, or until a toothpick inserted in the center comes out clean.
9. Let cool completely in the pan and serve.

Cheesecake Wontons

Servings: 6

Cooking Time: 16 Minutes

Ingredients:

- ¼ cup Regular or low-fat cream cheese (not fat-free)
- 2 tablespoons Granulated white sugar
- 1½ tablespoons Egg yolk
- ¼ teaspoon Vanilla extract
- ⅛ teaspoon Table salt
- 1½ tablespoons All-purpose flour
- 16 Wonton wrappers (vegetarian, if a concern)
- Vegetable oil spray

Directions:

1. Preheat the toaster oven to 400°F.
2. Using a flatware fork, mash the cream cheese, sugar, egg yolk, and vanilla in a small bowl until smooth. Add the salt and flour and continue mashing until evenly combined.
3. Set a wonton wrapper on a clean, dry work surface so that one corner faces you (so that it looks like a diamond on your work surface). Set 1 teaspoon of the cream cheese mixture in the middle of the wrapper but just above a horizontal line that would divide the wrapper in half. Dip your clean finger in water and run it along the edges of the wrapper. Fold the corner closest to you up and over the filling, lining it up with the corner farthest from you, thereby making a stuffed triangle. Press gently to seal. Wet the two triangle tips nearest you, then fold them up and together over the filling. Gently press together to seal and fuse. Set aside and continue making more stuffed wontons, 11 more for the small

batch, 15 more for the medium batch, or 23 more for the large one.

4. Lightly coat the stuffed wrappers on all sides with vegetable oil spray. Set them with the fused corners up in the air fryer oven with as much air space between them as possible. Air-fry undisturbed for 6 minutes, or until golden brown and crisp.

5. Gently dump the contents of the air fryer oven onto a wire rack. Cool for at least 5 minutes before serving.

Chocolate Cupcakes With Salted Caramel Buttercream

Servings: 12

Cooking Time: 20 Minutes

Ingredients:

- Cake Ingredients
- 1 egg
- ½ cup vegetable oil
- ½ cup buttermilk
- ½ teaspoon vanilla extract
- 1 cup granulated sugar
- 1 cup all-purpose flour
- ¼ cup dark cocoa powder
- 1 teaspoon baking soda
- ½ teaspoon salt
- ½ teaspoon instant espresso powder
- ½ cup boiling water (205°-212°F)
- Buttercream Ingredients
- ½ cup unsalted butter, room temperature
- ⅓ cup caramel sauce, room temperature
- ½ teaspoon vanilla extract
- ½ teaspoon kosher salt
- 1 cup powdered sugar

Directions:

1. Whisk together the egg, vegetable oil, buttermilk, and vanilla extract in a bowl and set aside.
2. Sift together sugar, flour, cocoa powder, baking soda, salt, and instant espresso in a large mixing bowl.
3. Add the wet ingredients into the dry and mix until well combined.
4. Pour in the boiling water slowly while whisking vigorously until the batter is smooth.
5. Line the muffin pan with cupcake liners, then pour in the batter.
6. Preheat the toaster Oven to 350°F.
7. Place the cupcakes on the wire rack, then insert the rack at mid position in the preheated oven.
8. Select the Bake and Fan functions, adjust time to 20 minutes, and press Start/Pause.
9. Remove when done and allow cupcakes to cool on a wire rack for 2 hours.
10. Beat butter using a stand mixer on medium speed for 1 minute or until smooth and fluffy.
11. Beat in the caramel sauce, vanilla, and salt for 2 minutes or until well combined. You may need to scrape down the side of the bowl occasionally.
12. Add the powdered sugar slowly, beating on low speed until fully incorporated.
13. Beat the buttercream on medium speed for 2 minutes or until smooth and creamy.
14. Pipe the buttercream onto the cooled cupcake using a decorated tip.
15. Place the cakes in the fridge for 30 minutes before serving.

Spice Cake

Servings: 6

Cooking Time: 25 Minutes

Ingredients:

- 1 cup applesauce or 2 4-ounce jars baby food prunes
- ¼ cup skim milk or low-fat soy milk
- 1 tablespoon vegetable oil
- ½ cup brown sugar
- 1 egg
- 1½ cups unbleached flour
- 1 teaspoon baking powder
- ½ teaspoon baking soda
- ¼ teaspoon grated nutmeg
- ½ teaspoon ground cinnamon
- ½ teaspoon grated orange zest
- Salt to taste
- Creamy Frosting

Directions:

1. Preheat the toaster oven to 350° F.
2. Stir together the applesauce, milk, oil, sugar, and egg in a small bowl. Set aside.
3. Combine the flour, baking powder, nutmeg, cinnamon, orange zest, and salt in a medium bowl. Add the applesauce mixture and stir to mix well. Pour the batter into an oiled or nonstick 8½ × 8½ × 2-inch square baking (cake) pan.
4. BAKE for 25 minutes, or until a toothpick inserted in the center comes out clean. Frost with Creamy Frosting.

Almost Sinless Pear Banana Bread Pudding

Servings: 4

Cooking Time: 40 Minutes

Ingredients:

- 1 cup peeled and sliced fresh pears or 1 cup sliced canned pears, well drained
- 1 banana
- 1 cup skim milk
- 1 egg
- 2 tablespoons light brown sugar
- ¼ teaspoon salt ½ teaspoon ground cinnamon
- 2 cups toast, cut into 1 × 1-inch cubes or pieces

Directions:

1. Preheat the toaster oven to 400° F.
2. Blend the pears, banana, milk, egg, sugar, salt, and cinnamon in a food processor or blender until smooth. Transfer to an 8½ × 8½ × 4-inch ovenproof baking dish. Add the toast and mix well.
3. BAKE for 40 minutes, or until the center is firm and lightly browned. Cool and top with whipped cream, ice cream, nuts, or fresh or canned berries.

Chewy Coconut Cake

Servings: 6

Cooking Time: 22 Minutes

Ingredients:

- ¾ cup plus 2½ tablespoons All-purpose flour
- ¾ teaspoon Baking powder
- ⅛ teaspoon Table salt
- 7½ tablespoons (1 stick minus ½ tablespoon) Butter, at room temperature
- ⅓ cup plus 1 tablespoon Granulated white sugar
- 5 tablespoons Packed light brown sugar
- 5 tablespoons Pasteurized egg substitute, such as Egg Beaters
- 2 teaspoons Vanilla extract
- ½ cup Unsweetened shredded coconut

- Baking spray

Directions:

1. Preheat the toaster oven to 325°F.
2. Mix the flour, baking powder, and salt in a small bowl until well combined.
3. Using an electric hand mixer at medium speed , beat the butter, granulated white sugar, and brown sugar in a medium bowl until creamy and smooth, about 3 minutes, occasionally scraping down the inside of the bowl. Beat in the egg substitute or egg and vanilla until smooth.
4. Scrape down and remove the beaters. Fold in the flour mixture with a rubber spatula just until all the flour is moistened. Fold in the coconut until the mixture is a uniform color.
5. Use the baking spray to generously coat the inside of a 6-inch round cake pan for a small batch, a 7-inch round cake pan for a medium batch, or an 8-inch round cake pan for a large batch. Scrape and spread the batter into the pan, smoothing the batter out to an even layer.
6. Set the pan in the toaster oven and air-fry for 18 minutes for a 6-inch layer, 20 minutes for a 7-inch layer, or 22 minutes for an 8-inch layer, or until the cake is well browned and set even if there's a little soft give right at the center. Start checking it at the 16-minute mark to know where you are.
7. Use hot pads or silicone baking mitts to transfer the cake pan to a wire rack. Cool for at least 1 hour or up to 4 hours. Use a nonstick-safe knife to slice the cake into wedges right in the pan, lifting them out one by one.

Dark Chocolate Peanut Butter S'mores

Servings: 4

Cooking Time: 6 Minutes

Ingredients:

- 4 graham cracker sheets
- 4 marshmallows
- 4 teaspoons chunky peanut butter
- 4 ounces dark chocolate
- ½ teaspoon ground cinnamon

Directions:

1. Preheat the toaster oven to 390°F. Break the graham crackers in half so you have 8 pieces.
2. Place 4 pieces of graham cracker on the bottom of the air fryer oven. Top each with one of the marshmallows and bake for 6 or 7 minutes, or until the marshmallows have a golden brown center.
3. While cooking, slather each of the remaining graham crackers with 1 teaspoon peanut butter.
4. When baking completes, carefully remove each of the graham crackers, add 1 ounce of dark chocolate on top of the marshmallow, and lightly sprinkle with cinnamon. Top with the remaining peanut butter graham cracker to make the sandwich. Serve immediately.

Honey-roasted Mixed Nuts

Servings: 8

Cooking Time: 15 Minutes

Ingredients:

- ½ cup raw, shelled pistachios
- ½ cup raw almonds
- 1 cup raw walnuts
- 2 tablespoons filtered water
- 2 tablespoons honey
- 1 tablespoon vegetable oil
- 2 tablespoons sugar
- ½ teaspoon salt

Directions:

1. Preheat the toaster oven to 300°F.
2. Lightly spray an air-fryer-safe pan with olive oil; then place the pistachios, almonds, and walnuts inside the pan and place the pan inside the air fryer oven.
3. Air-fry for 15 minutes, every 5 minutes to rotate the nuts.
4. While the nuts are roasting, boil the water in a small pan and stir in the honey and oil. Continue to stir while cooking until the water begins to evaporate and a thick sauce is formed. The sauce should stick to the back of a wooden spoon when mixed. Turn off the heat.
5. Remove the nuts from the air fryer oven (cooking should have just completed) and spoon the nuts into the stovetop pan. Use a spatula to coat the nuts with the honey syrup.
6. Line a baking sheet with parchment paper and spoon the nuts onto the sheet. Lightly sprinkle the sugar and salt over the nuts and let cool in the refrigerator for at least 2 hours.
7. When the honey and sugar have hardened, store the nuts in an airtight container in the refrigerator.

German Chocolate Cake

Servings: 6

Cooking Time: 25 Minutes

Ingredients:

- Butter, shortening, or nonstick cooking spray
- ⅔ cup whole milk
- ½ teaspoon white vinegar
- ⅔ cup all-purpose flour
- 3 tablespoons unsweetened cocoa powder
- ½ teaspoon baking soda
- ½ teaspoon baking powder
- ¼ teaspoon table salt
- ½ cup packed dark brown sugar
- 2 tablespoons canola or vegetable oil
- 1 large egg
- ½ teaspoon pure vanilla extract
- GERMAN CHOCOLATE FROSTING
- 1 large egg yolk
- ½ cup evaporated milk
- ⅓ cup granulated sugar
- 3 tablespoons unsalted butter
- ¾ cup sweetened flaked coconut
- ⅓ cup chopped pecans, toasted

Directions:

1. Preheat the toaster oven to 350°F. Line an 8-inch round cake pan with parchment paper and lightly grease the bottom and sides with butter or shortening or spray with nonstick cooking spray.
2. Pour the milk into a medium bowl and stir in the vinegar; set aside.
3. Whisk the flour, cocoa, baking soda, baking powder, and salt in a small bowl; set aside.
4. Whisk the brown sugar, oil, egg, and vanilla in a medium bowl. Add the flour mixture, in thirds, alternately with the milk mixture, beginning and ending with the flour. Blend well and scrape the sides of the bowl as needed.
5. Pour the batter into the prepared pan. Bake for 20 to 25 minutes, or until a wooden pick inserted into the center comes out clean. Let cool on a wire rack for 10 minutes. Invert onto a serving platter and allow to cool completely.
6. Make the frosting: Combine the egg yolk, evaporated milk, sugar, and butter in a small saucepan. Cook, stirring, over medium heat for about 6 minutes or until thickened and bubbly. Remove from the heat and stir in the coconut and pecans. Cover and let cool completely. Frost the top of the cake.

Rum-glazed Roasted Pineapple

Servings: 4

Cooking Time: 45 Minutes

Ingredients:

- ½ pineapple, peeled, cored, and cut lengthwise into 4 wedges
- 2 tablespoons unsalted butter, melted
- 3 tablespoons packed dark brown sugar
- 1 tablespoon lime juice
- ½ teaspoon vanilla extract
- Pinch table salt
- 1 tablespoon white or aged rum
- 2 tablespoons unsweetened shredded coconut, toasted

Directions:

1. Adjust toaster oven rack to lowest position and preheat the toaster oven to 450 degrees. Toss pineapple with melted butter in 8-inch square baking dish or pan, then arrange in single layer. Roast until bottoms of wedges are deep golden brown and fork slips easily in and out of pineapple, 25 to 35 minutes, rotating dish halfway through roasting.
2. Remove pan from oven and transfer pineapple to serving dish. Whisk sugar, lime juice, vanilla, and salt into butter and juice in pan, scraping up any browned bits, until well combined. Return pineapple wedges to pan, browned side up, along with any accumulated juices. Roast until sauce is reduced to syrupy consistency, 3 to 5 minutes.
3. Remove pan from oven and transfer pineapple to serving dish. Whisk rum into sauce in pan until smooth, then spoon sauce over pineapple. Sprinkle with coconut and serve.

Fried Oreos

Servings: 12

Cooking Time: 7 Minutes

Ingredients:

- 1 Large egg white(s)
- 2 tablespoons Water
- 1 cup Graham cracker crumbs
- 12 Original-size Oreos (not minis or king-size)
- Vegetable oil spray

Directions:

1. Preheat the toaster oven to 375°F .
2. Set up and fill two shallow soup plates or small pie plates on your counter: one for the egg white(s), whisked with the water until foamy; and one for the graham cracker crumbs.
3. Dip a cookie in the egg white mixture, turning several times to coat well. Let any excess egg white mixture slip back into the rest, then set the cookie in the crumbs. Turn several times to coat evenly, pressing gently. You want an even but not thick crust. However, make sure that the cookie is fully coated and that the filling is sealed inside. Lightly coat the cookie on all sides with vegetable oil spray. Set aside and continue dipping and coating the remaining cookies.
4. Set the coated cookies in the oven with as much air space between them as possible. Air-fry undisturbed for 6 minutes, or until the coating is golden brown and set. If the machine is at 360°F, the cookies may need 1 minute more to cook and set.
5. Use a nonstick-safe spatula to transfer the cookies to a wire rack. Cool for at least 5 minutes before serving.

Giant Buttery Oatmeal Cookie

Servings: 4

Cooking Time: 16 Minutes

Ingredients:

- 1 cup Rolled oats (not quick-cooking or steel-cut oats)
- ½ cup All-purpose flour
- ½ teaspoon Baking soda
- ½ teaspoon Ground cinnamon
- ½ teaspoon Table salt
- 3½ tablespoons Butter, at room temperature
- ⅓ cup Packed dark brown sugar
- 1½ tablespoons Granulated white sugar
- 3 tablespoons (or 1 medium egg, well beaten) Pasteurized egg substitute, such as Egg Beaters
- ¾ teaspoon Vanilla extract
- ⅓ cup Chopped pecans
- Baking spray

Directions:

1. Preheat the toaster oven to 350°F.
2. Stir the oats, flour, baking soda, cinnamon, and salt in a bowl until well combined.
3. Using an electric hand mixer at medium speed , beat the butter, brown sugar, and granulated white sugar until creamy and thick, about 3 minutes, scraping down the inside of the bowl occasionally. Beat in the egg substitute or egg (as applicable) and vanilla until uniform.
4. Scrape down and remove the beaters. Fold in the flour mixture and pecans with a rubber spatula just until all the flour is moistened and the nuts are even throughout the dough.
5. For a small air fryer oven, coat the inside of a 6-inch round cake pan with baking spray. For a medium air fryer oven, coat the inside of a 7-inch round cake pan with baking spray. And for a large air fryer oven, coat the inside of an 8-inch round cake pan with baking spray. Scrape and gently press the dough into the prepared pan, spreading it into an even layer to the perimeter.
6. Set the pan in the toaster oven and air-fry undisturbed for 16 minutes, or until puffed and browned.
7. Transfer the pan to a wire rack and cool for 10 minutes. Loosen the cookie from the perimeter with a spatula, then invert the pan onto a cutting board and let the cookie come free. Remove the pan and reinvert the cookie onto the wire rack. Cool for 5 minutes more before slicing into wedges to serve.

Gingerbread

Servings: 6

Cooking Time: 20 Minutes

Ingredients:

- cooking spray
- 1 cup flour
- 2 tablespoons sugar
- ¾ teaspoon ground ginger
- ¼ teaspoon cinnamon
- 1 teaspoon baking powder
- ½ teaspoon baking soda
- ⅛ teaspoon salt
- 1 egg
- ¼ cup molasses
- ½ cup buttermilk
- 2 tablespoons oil
- 1 teaspoon pure vanilla extract

Directions:

1. Preheat the toaster oven to 330°F.
2. Spray 6 x 6-inch baking dish lightly with cooking spray.
3. In a medium bowl, mix together all the dry ingredients.

4. In a separate bowl, beat the egg. Add molasses, buttermilk, oil, and vanilla and stir until well mixed.
5. Pour liquid mixture into dry ingredients and stir until well blended.
6. Pour batter into baking dish and Air-fry at 330°F for 20 minutes or until toothpick inserted in center of loaf comes out clean.

Apple Strudel

Servings: 2
Cooking Time: 90 Minutes

Ingredients:

- 2 Golden Delicious apples (14 ounces), peeled, cored, and cut into ½-inch pieces
- 1½ tablespoons granulated sugar
- ¼ teaspoon grated lemon zest plus 1 teaspoon juice
- ⅛ teaspoon ground cinnamon
- ⅛ teaspoon ground ginger
- ⅛ teaspoon table salt, divided
- 2 tablespoons golden raisins
- 1 tablespoon panko bread crumbs
- 3½ tablespoons unsalted butter, melted
- 1½ teaspoons confectioners' sugar, plus extra for serving
- 7 (14 by 9-inch) phyllo sheets, thawed

Directions:

1. Toss apples, granulated sugar, lemon zest and juice, cinnamon, ginger, and pinch salt together in large bowl. Cover and microwave until apples are softened, 2 to 4 minutes, stirring once halfway through microwaving. Let apples sit, covered, for 5 minutes. Transfer apples to colander set in second large bowl and let drain, reserving liquid. Return apples to bowl; stir in raisins and panko.
2. Adjust toaster oven rack to middle position and preheat the toaster oven to 350 degrees. Spray small rimmed baking sheet with vegetable oil spray. Stir remaining pinch salt into melted butter.
3. Place 16½ by 12-inch sheet of parchment paper on counter with long side parallel to edge of counter. Place 1 phyllo sheet on parchment with long side parallel to edge of counter. Place confectioners' sugar in fine-mesh strainer. Lightly brush sheet with melted butter and dust sparingly with confectioners' sugar. Repeat with remaining 6 phyllo sheets, melted butter, and confectioners' sugar, stacking sheets one on top of other as you go.
4. Arrange apple mixture in 2½ by 10-inch rectangle 2 inches from bottom of phyllo and about 2 inches from each side. Using parchment, fold sides of phyllo over filling, then fold bottom edge of phyllo over filling. Brush folded portions of phyllo with reserved apple liquid. Fold top edge over filling, making sure top and bottom edges overlap by about 1 inch. (If they do not overlap, unfold, rearrange filling into slightly narrower strip, and refold.) Press firmly to seal. Using thin metal spatula, transfer strudel to prepared sheet. Lightly brush top and sides of strudel with remaining apple liquid.
5. Bake until golden brown, 25 to 30 minutes, rotating sheet halfway through baking. Using thin metal spatula, immediately transfer strudel to cutting board. Let cool for 3 minutes. Slice strudel and let cool for at least 20 minutes. Serve warm or at room temperature, dusting with extra confectioners' sugar before serving.

Not Key Lime, Lime Pie

Servings: 3

Cooking Time: 27 Minutes

Ingredients:

- 1 tablespoon grated lime zest
- 3 large egg yolks
- 1 (14-ounce) can sweetened condensed milk
- ½ cup fresh lime juice
- 1 ¾ cups graham cracker crumbs (about 12 full graham crackers)
- ⅓ cup granulated sugar
- ⅛ teaspoon table salt
- ½ cup unsalted butter, melted
- Nonstick cooking spray
- WHIPPED CREAM
- 1 cup heavy cream
- ⅓ cup confectioners' sugar

Directions:

1. Preheat the toaster oven to 350°F.
2. Whisk the lime zest and egg yolks in a large bowl for 1 minute. Whisk in the sweetened condensed milk and lime juice. Set aside to thicken while you prepare the crust.
3. Stir the graham cracker crumbs, granulated sugar, and salt in a medium bowl. Pour the butter over the mixture and mix until combined and moist. Press the crust evenly into the bottom and up the sides of a 9-inch pie plate. Pack tightly using the back of a large spoon. Bake for 10 minutes. Let cool on a cooling rack.
4. When the crust is completely cool, pour the lime filling inside. Bake for 15 to 17 minutes, or until the center is set (it will still jiggle a bit). Allow the pie to cool completely at room temperature. Spray plastic wrap with nonstick cooking spray and place on the pie. Refrigerate for at least 3 hours or overnight.
5. Beat the cream in a large bowl with an electric mixer at medium-high speed until soft peaks form. Add the confectioners' sugar, one tablespoon at a time, and continue to beat until stiff peaks form. Dollop, pipe, or spread the whipped cream over the pie before serving. Refrigerate leftovers for up to 3 days.

Soft Peanut Butter Cookies

Servings: 12

Cooking Time: 20 Minutes

Ingredients:

- 1/2 cup vegetable shortening
- 1/2 cup peanut butter
- 1 1/4 cups light brown sugar
- 1 egg
- 1 teaspoon vanilla
- 1/2 teaspoon salt
- 1 1/2 cups flour
- 1 teaspoon baking soda
- Sugar crystals

Directions:

1. Preheat the toaster oven to 275°F.
2. Using the flat beater attachment, beat shortening, peanut butter, brown sugar, egg, and vanilla at a medium setting until well blended.
3. Reduce speed to low and gradually add dry ingredients until blended. Dough will be crumbly.
4. Roll 3 tablespoon-size portions of the dough into a ball. Place on ungreased cookie sheet.
5. Press to 1/2-inch thick. Sprinkle with sugar crystals.
6. Bake 18 to 20 minutes. Do not overcook.

Baked Custard

Servings: 2
Cooking Time: 45 Minutes

Ingredients:

- 2 eggs
- ¼ cup sugar
- 1 cup low-fat evaporated milk
- ½ teaspoon vanilla extract
- Pinch of grated nutmeg
- Fat-free half-and-half

Directions:

1. Preheat the toaster oven to 350° F.
2. Beat together the eggs, sugar, milk, vanilla, and nutmeg in a small bowl with an electric mixer at medium speed. Pour equal portions of the custard mixture into 2 oiled 1-cup-size ovenproof dishes.
3. BAKE for 45 minutes, or until a toothpick inserted in the center comes out clean. Serve drizzled with warm fat-free half-and-half.

Chocolate And Vanilla Swirled Pudding

Servings: 4
Cooking Time: 25 Minutes

Ingredients:

- 1 square semisweet chocolate
- 1½ cups fat-free half-and-half
- 1 tablespoon sugar
- 2 egg yolks
- ½ teaspoon vanilla extract
- Fat-free whipped topping

Directions:

1. Melt the chocolate in an oiled or nonstick 8½ × 8½ × 2-inch square baking (cake) pan under the broiler for approximately 5 minutes, removing the pan from the oven before the chocolate is completely melted. Stir until melted and smooth. Set aside.
2. Whisk together the half-and-half, sugar, egg yolks, and vanilla in a medium bowl. Divide into two portions and add the melted chocolate to one, stirring to blend well.
3. Fill four 1-cup-size ovenproof dishes with equal portions of the vanilla mixture, then top with equal portions of the chocolate mixture. With a skewer or toothpick, stir the pudding in little circles to create a swirling pattern of light and dark.
4. BAKE at 350° F. for 25 minutes, or until the pudding is firm. Chill before serving. Top with fat-free whipped topping.

Green Grape Meringues

Servings: 4
Cooking Time: 40 Minutes

Ingredients:

- 1 cup sugar
- 3 egg whites, beaten until stiff
- ½ teaspoon lemon juice
- Vanilla frozen yogurt
- 1 cup sliced fresh green grapes
- 2 squares unsweetened baking chocolate, shaved
- Nonfat whipped topping

Directions:

1. Preheat the toaster oven to 250° F.
2. Add the sugar slowly to the egg white mixture and continue to beat. Add the lemon juice. With a tablespoon, drop on an oiled or nonstick 6½ × 10-inch baking sheet to make a mound of meringue approximately 2 inches across. Make a slight depression in the center of each one.

3. BAKE for 40 minutes, or until crusty and browned. Cool and fill each meringue shell with a scoop of vanilla frozen yogurt. Top with equal portions of green grapes, chocolate shavings, and nonfat whipped topping. The meringues may be stored in an airtight container until ready to use.

Brown Sugar Baked Apples

Servings: 4
Cooking Time: 15 Minutes

Ingredients:

- 3 Small tart apples, preferably McIntosh
- 4 tablespoons (¼ cup/½ stick) Butter
- 6 tablespoons Light brown sugar
- Ground cinnamon
- Table salt

Directions:

1. Preheat the toaster oven to 400°F.
2. Stem the apples, then cut them in half through their "equators" (that is, not the stem ends). Use a melon baller to core the apples, taking care not to break through the flesh and skin at any point but creating a little well in the center of each half.
3. When the machine is at temperature, remove the baking pan and set it on a heat-safe work surface. Set the apple halves cut side up in the baking pan with as much air space between them as possible. Even a fraction of an inch will work. Drop 2 teaspoons of butter into the well in the center of each apple half. Sprinkle each half with 1 tablespoon brown sugar and a pinch each ground cinnamon and table salt.
4. Return the baking pan to the machine. Air-fry undisturbed for 15 minutes, or until the apple halves have softened and the brown sugar has caramelized.
5. Use a nonstick-safe spatula to transfer the apple halves cut side up to a wire rack. Cool for at least 10 minutes before serving, or serve at room temperature.

Freezer-to-oven Chocolate Chip Cookies

Servings: 6
Cooking Time: 15 Minutes

Ingredients:

- 2 ½ cups all-purpose flour
- 1 teaspoon baking soda
- ½ teaspoon table salt
- ¼ teaspoon baking powder
- 1 cup unsalted butter, softened
- 1 cup packed dark brown sugar
- ¾ cup granulated sugar
- 2 large eggs
- 2 teaspoons pure vanilla extract
- 1 (12-ounce) package semisweet chocolate chips

Directions:

1. Preheat the toaster oven to 375°F. Line a 12 x 12-inch baking sheet with parchment paper.
2. Whisk the flour, baking soda, salt, and baking powder in a medium bowl; set aside.
3. Beat the butter, brown sugar, and granulated sugar in a large bowl with a handheld mixer at medium-high speed for 2 minutes or until creamy. Beat in the eggs, one at a time, beating well after each addition. Beat in the vanilla. Mix in the dry ingredients until blended. Stir in the chocolate chips.
4. Using a 2-tablespoon scoop, shape the batter into balls about 1 ½ inches in diameter. Arrange the cookies 1 inch apart on the prepared baking sheet. Bake for 13 to 15 minutes or until golden brown. Remove from the oven and let cool for 1 minute, then transfer the cookies to a wire rack.

Frozen Brazo De Mercedes

Servings: 8

Cooking Time: 15 Minutes

Ingredients:

- 1 pint vanilla ice cream, softened to room temperature
- 1 (8 inch) premade graham cracker crust
- 6 large eggs, yolks and whites separated
- 7 ounces condensed milk
- ½ teaspoon vanilla extract
- ¼ teaspoon cream of tartar
- ⅓ cup granulated sugar

Directions:

1. Spread the ice cream on the bottom of the graham cracker crust in an even layer, cover with plastic wrap, and place in the freezer for 8 hours or overnight.
2. Whisk egg yolks and condensed milk over a double boiler continuously for 15 minutes or until the mixture becomes thick.
3. Whisk the vanilla extract into the egg mixture until fully combined.
4. Pass the custard through a fine sieve to remove any clumps.
5. Remove the ice cream and top with the egg yolk mixture, cover with plastic wrap, and place back into the freezer for 2 hours.
6. Beat the egg whites and cream of tartar in a stand mixer on high speed.
7. Add the sugar in slowly once the egg whites begin to foam.
8. Beat the egg whites for two minutes or until they form stiff peaks.
9. Remove the plastic wrap from the pie and top with the beaten egg whites.
10. Preheat the toaster Oven to 350°F.
11. Place the pie on the wire rack, then insert the rack at mid position in the preheated air fryer.
12. Select the Bake and Shake functions, adjust time to 15 minutes, and press Start/Pause.
13. Rotate the pie halfway through cooking for even browning. The Shake Reminder will let you know when.
14. Remove when done and place in the fridge for 1 hour, uncovered.
15. Cover the pie, then place in the freezer for 6 hours or overnight.
16. Remove the pie and allow it to rest at room temperature for 10 minutes, then slice and serve.

Triple Chocolate Brownies

Servings: 16

Cooking Time: 25 Minutes

Ingredients:

- ⅓ cup salted butter, room temperature, plus extra for greasing the baking dish
- ¾ cup brown sugar
- 2 large eggs
- 1 teaspoon vanilla extract
- ½ cup all-purpose flour
- ¼ cup cocoa powder
- ¼ teaspoon baking powder
- ⅛ teaspoon salt
- ½ cup dark chocolate chips
- ¼ cup white chocolate chips

Directions:

1. Place the rack in position 1 and preheat the oven to 325°F on BAKE for 5 minutes.
2. Lightly grease a 6-inch-square baking dish with butter.
3. In a large bowl, beat together the butter and sugar with an electric hand beater or a whisk until

combined. Add the eggs and vanilla and beat to combine.

4. Beat in the flour, cocoa powder, baking powder, and salt until just combined.
5. Stir in dark chocolate and white chocolate chips, then spoon the batter into the prepared dish.
6. Bake for 25 minutes or until a knife inserted in the center comes out mostly clean.
7. Cool in the baking dish and serve.

White Chocolate Cranberry Blondies

Servings: 6

Cooking Time: 18 Minutes

Ingredients:

- ⅓ cup butter
- ½ cup sugar
- 1 teaspoon vanilla extract
- 1 large egg
- 1 cup all-purpose flour
- ½ teaspoon baking powder
- ⅛ teaspoon salt
- ¼ cup dried cranberries
- ¼ cup white chocolate chips

Directions:

1. Preheat the toaster oven to 320°F.
2. In a large bowl, cream the butter with the sugar and vanilla extract. Whisk in the egg and set aside.
3. In a separate bowl, mix the flour with the baking powder and salt. Then gently mix the dry ingredients into the wet. Fold in the cranberries and chocolate chips.
4. Liberally spray an oven-safe 7-inch springform pan with olive oil and pour the batter into the pan.
5. Air-fry for 17 minutes or until a toothpick inserted in the center comes out clean.
6. Remove and let cool 5 minutes before serving.

RECIPE INDEX

CPSIA information can be obtained
at www.ICGtesting.com
Printed in the USA
LVHW101144310821
696548LV00005B/75

9 781803 209876